MANUFACTURING PROGRESS

MANUFACTURING PROGRESS

In the Post-COVID Era

Nicholas Dionysius
Julius Storozynski

NEW DEGREE PRESS

COPYRIGHT © 2021 NICHOLAS DIONYSIUS JULIUS STOROZYNSKI

All rights reserved.

MANUFACTURING PROGRESS

In the Post-COVID Era

ISBN

978-1-63676-842-7   *Paperback*

978-1-63730-200-2   *Kindle Ebook*

978-1-63730-286-6   *Digital Ebook*

To Bella. Carry the fire.

CONTENTS

	AUTHOR'S NOTE	11
CHAPTER 1	WHAT DO YOU THINK ARE THE THREE BIGGEST PROBLEMS FACING AMERICA TODAY?	17
CHAPTER 2	SAME TEAM	33
CHAPTER 3	STRATEGIC INITIATIVES: PLAYING THE LONG GAME	47
CHAPTER 4	MAULED BY BLUE CROSS	61
CHAPTER 5	WELCOME TO THE JUNGLE	77
CHAPTER 6	CONSCIOUS OF CLASS	89
CHAPTER 7	GILDED AGE MERRY-GO-ROUND: THE BIG, SEXY ECON CHAPTER	93
CHAPTER 8	SPLIT DOWN THE MIDDLE: DEMAND-SIDE JESUS	109
CHAPTER 9	WHAT'S THE WORST THAT COULD HAPPEN?	127
CHAPTER 10	PROGRESSIVES AS THE SOLUTION	139
CHAPTER 11	DO YOU WANT TO WIN ARGUMENTS OR DO YOU WANT TO MAKE THE WORLD A BETTER PLACE?	159
	ACKNOWLEDGMENTS	165
	APPENDIX	169

Za naszą i waszą wolność

For our freedom and yours

—TADEUSZ KOSCIUSZKO

AUTHOR'S NOTE

There's a growing consensus that something, or everything, in American politics is going wrong.

For those of us who were Obama Democrats, it seems this sand in the gears has just blown in. Sure, things have changed. You could credibly say this change started during the Reagan years, or that things started spiraling out of control with the Newt Gingrich-led impeachment and government shutdown, or that George W. Bush was the true end of America's heroic world leadership. Ok, fine—some might say that things were good until opinion pieces like those by Bill O'Reilly or Sean Hannity began masquerading as news and ended civility in our national discourse. But definitely, absolutely, the last time things were on the rails was 2016. Promise.

There's a great case to be made for each, so the one I would point to in casual conversation is usually the last one I was thinking about, in much the same way that my favorite Tarantino movie is whichever one I've seen most recently (currently The Hateful Eight). No matter which one we discuss, therefore, I would tend to agree.

For those further to the left than Obama-style Democrats, the belief is that this system was designed to run with sand in the gears. America was built on slavery and stolen ground, dragged its feet through Reconstruction, and didn't pass the Civil Rights Act until peaceful protests turned to riots after Dr. King's assassination, or so the argument goes. Or maybe it's the system of capitalism itself, based upon the exploitation of the working class, and expanding across the globe for sweatshops in Asia, wars for oil in the Middle East, and coups in Bolivia to ensure dirt-cheap prices for the rare metals found in Tesla batteries.

Well, when you point out all the atrocities like that, it's hard to disagree.

There's an old saying that "Someone who is nice to me, but not to the waiter, isn't a nice person." For those people, America is a diner who insulted the waiter, left no tip, and then followed him out to the parking lot to knock him out and steal the gas money from his wallet.

Debating between one or the other is wasting time from implementing real change. It's possible to admit that some things are built into the system and try to change them and to admit that things have gotten worse at some point in the last forty years. Thinking critically about which things have gotten worse is not only an important question unto itself but will speak to greater themes of injustice baked into the system. You can point to the fact that the War on Drugs targeted people of color, which is bad and then see a greater trend of racial injustice. You can point to the fact that cutting taxes on the wealthy leads to gross income inequality, which is bad, and then see a greater trend of economic injustice.

Let's start by asking ourselves: What exactly is going wrong, and when did this start? What did the world look like before that was the case? For at least forty years following the 1940s, America had low unemployment, lower inequality, a big social safety net, a minimum wage equivalent to $22 an hour in 2020, and a president pushing for all Americans to have access to affordable health care. Hell, there was even a time when a Republican president said that any dollar spent on war and bullets was a dollar that could be used to feed a hungry child. How do we shift the Overton window back in that direction?

(For those who would throw the baby out with the bathwater because America was built on stolen land, there are problems inherent to capitalism:

1. I'm not a priest, but I don't think you can give confession to an abstract notion like a nation.

2. I'm too shy to write a Revolutions for Dummies book but let me know how that goes.)

I started writing this book because I wanted to learn why liberals are so bad at talking about important issues and even worse at winning elections. I was frustrated by the fact that liberals didn't have a big picture strategy capable of beating a reality TV show host and a slew of conspiracy theorists. It then evolved into a reflection on the most important questions facing us as a nation:

What does an America that works for everyone look like?

Writing helped to organize and gather my thoughts. Hopefully, it will make my worldview make sense to someone who doesn't agree with me and change their mind for the better.

The title of this book is a reference to Manufacturing Consent by Edward S. Herman and Noam Chomsky. The main idea of the book is that the media serves in part to make people want things they wouldn't normally want. In the lead-up to the Iraq War, for example, even the New York Times was writing op-eds and phrasing their articles in a way that made the war seem inevitable, which warms people up to the idea of going to war. Normal people didn't really have anything to gain from going to war, but the media helped them to think that something bad was good for them. I want to do the opposite here and use my voice to help people realize they are allowed to demand better treatment. This is my small part to manufacture some progress in the right direction for our country. You pay your taxes, and you are allowed to want a government to work for you.

This book aims to hijack that same mechanism but by manufacturing support for progressive policies. We should be asking if $1,200 a month is enough to help our people or if we need to go to $3,000 a month. We should be demanding the money we use on missiles go to giving Medicare to all of our citizens. We should be holding our elected officials responsible for getting our money's worth out of our tax dollars. That's Progress.

So, here's my attempt to talk about where we are as a nation, to stitch together where we can go forward. My audience aren't wonks, partly because in-depth policy detail doesn't change minds, but mostly because wonks throw terrible parties. My audience is people who vote, people who might vote but don't, the heroes who talk to the first two groups of individuals, and people who might run for office or guide the conversation in those offices.

For people who vote: I will make a case for why these progressive policies aren't as crazy as they seem and will improve your lives. Push your representatives toward these positions.

For people with different beliefs than I have: I will explain why I see the world the way I do and nudge you toward considering progressive voices. At the very least, I'll have you laugh along at some (intentional) jokes.

For the politicos reading this, let me just say: Madame Speaker, what an honor! Nothing would give me greater pleasure than to have you run on these issues and guide the conversation while boosting your career.

Finally, for people canvassing or getting out the vote: I'll share some lines and points I think might help you find success, as well as kiss you on the top of the head and tell you how proud I am of you.

Law is boring, and economics is boring, but they're both too important to leave to the lawyers and the economists.

Let's make it sexy.

CHAPTER 1

WHAT DO YOU THINK ARE THE THREE BIGGEST PROBLEMS FACING AMERICA TODAY?

———

You can tell a lot about a person by the way they answer the question.

It's a question of priorities and values. This is the simplest way I've learned to ask, "What are your values as an American citizen?" I ask myself this pretty frequently. It helps make sure you're paying attention.

Obviously, there are going to be people on your Facebook feed telling you that the biggest problem facing America is somehow a social justice group like Black Lives Matter and assuring you that this group is a domestic terror threat on par with the Ku Klux Klan, only worse because it's founded by George Soros and they just take that money and send it to the Democratic Party. These kinds of racist-flavored social media rants might make you regret considering the question.

But then again, it's still a useful question because, in one sentence, you just found out that their number one American value is racism. How efficient!

In more normal conversations, you may get a very broad answer to an admittedly broad question. "Trumpism," for example, seems to be an all-encompassing answer, ranging from "The former president is an orange buffoon," to "Our systems of law are being eroded, paving the way for fascism," to "I'm not sure, I don't usually pay attention to politics, but something about this whole situation is off." This is the kind of answer that requires digging deeper.

My first job out of college was a sales role at a large tech company. As a driven young man seeking success, I'd ask all kinds of people about their work and ended up with a very useful piece of advice from someone who worked at a car dealership:

"Always clarify. Different words mean different things to different people. Take the word safety, for example. When someone comes in, and you ask what they're looking for in a car and they tell you safety, that could mean that they want a tank of a car that will withstand any crash to something super sporty that's fast enough in the hands of a good driver to avoid any collision."

While Trump is out of office, Trumpism seems like it has some staying power as senators adopt his rhetoric and QAnon conspiracy theorists have won races across the country. However, running against Trumpism didn't guarantee Democratic down-ballot wins in 2020 and isn't likely to do so in the future (Democrats lost seats in the House and in state legislatures).

Maybe fear of his legacy will actually solve all of the world's ills, and we can get back to pretending everything is fine like we were in 2015.

I'm not hopeful, but you know. Maybe.

This isn't to say that fears of authoritarianism and overreach aren't valid. The January 6th riots at the Capitol let the genie out of the bottle, spurred on by sitting senators and members of the House. During Trump's tenure, the Department of Justice used its lawyers to go after a woman who credibly accused Trump of rape in the 1990s. Bill Barr, head of the Department of Justice, used his office to downplay the Russia Dossier and delayed the report to ensure people forgot about it, which they essentially did. The Senate voted to acquit Trump after his first and second impeachments and buried its own investigation into election interference in the 2016 race. These are just the things we know about.

But you know what? Most citizens who aren't MSNBC or FOX junkies are disconnected from these issues. Big government, for most people, means something like a mask mandate, rather than the National Security Agency tapping our phones.

We all got a civics lesson on how our government works just from hearing about these issues in the news and having smart people disseminate this information through social media and . . . our only option is to vote? Again, I'm not writing a How-To Revolution guide here. I'll save that for my next volume, A Citizen's Guide to Guillotine Maintenance. A general strike would be powerful, but if a year of pandemic-exposed economic injustice and secret police forces in Portland didn't provoke it, you have to wonder what will.

Every so often, my dad will call me, asking, "Can you believe . . ." followed by a rant of things that not only can I not believe, but I have no idea how to make actionable items out of. I can't call up Ted Cruz and force him to apologize for egging on the January 6th riots.

These are the jobs of our bureaucrats, and the only option I can think of is to help people think of how to find better bureaucrats. To that end, I want politicians who actually share my values, and the only way I can know that for sure is if they support policies I believe in. Life would be much easier if the solution were always "Vote Democrat," but most Democrats didn't put up much of a fight over Trump's military budget, and Joe Biden is still keeping kids in cages.

If "Vote Blue No Matter Who" doesn't work, what values do I look for? Here are my big three issues:

INEQUALITY
We are the richest nation in the history of the world. Many of our citizens have lives that would make kings from a thousand years ago look like absolute chumps. Life, for many, is good and is only getting better.

Eight of our citizens own more wealth than half of the rest of the world.[1] On the other hand, one in eleven children in America lives in poverty.[2] More than half a million people are experiencing homelessness.[3] Poor people were significantly more likely to catch COVID-19 and significantly more likely to die from it when they caught it.[4] The majority of Americans think their children will grow up to be poorer than their parents.[5]

Philosopher John Rawls thought that inequality in society could only be justified if any other alternative world would leave the less fortunate worse off than they were to begin with it.[6] You can hear echoes of this today when you hear people say that Jeff Bezos having a personal wealth of $200 billion makes us all better off. Even though it would only cost him $11 billion to end world hunger by some estimates, it's good for society that he's allowed to have so much more money than the rest of us.[7]

The real danger that people don't often speak of, however, is the fact that the ultrawealthy have the power to damage our democracy.

---

1 Curtin, "Meet the 8 Men."
2 Haider, "The Basic Facts."
3 Smiljanic, "Homelessness Statistics."
4 Goldstein, "Income Emerges."
5 Fottrell, "Most Americans."
6 Wenar, "John Rawls."
7 "Ending World Hunger," International Institute for Sustainable Development.

I'd like to clarify here that I'm not talking about run-of-the-mill rich people. It's all well and good that someone can create a successful business and be rewarded with enough to provide for their family several times over. Having the motivation for getting wealthy has led to the development of consumer products that make American life so cushy. I'm talking about the billionaire class.

Consider Mike Bloomberg's vanity run for Democratic presidential candidate. All told, Little Mike spent half a billion dollars between cable advertisements (spending so much that channels like MSNBC and CNN essentially had to give him positive coverage at risk of damaging their bottom line), campaign contributions to other politicians (turns out if you give a random congressman $3 million they'll endorse you, and if you do this a bunch of times you'll get a bunch of endorsements; who knew?) and online advertisements (to the point that "Mike paid me to make this meme" became a meme).[8] He spent so much money that paying for good coverage turned into organic good coverage as people bought into the hype . . . until he got on stage and Americans who had never heard his voice got bored and left. If Bloomberg had a shred of charisma, he would likely have been the Democratic nominee instead of Joe Biden.

All of this, by the way, made no difference in his quality of life. Mike spent half a billion dollars and nearly bought his way into the presidency and didn't even have to make the switch to buying socks at Costco.

---

8   Hee Lee, "Does Money Even Matter?"

Now consider the fact that the average senate seat win cost around $15 million in 2018.[9] Within a few years, Mike could buy fifty-one senators for cheaper than it was for him to get drop-kicked by Elizabeth Warren on live TV. Ditto the roughly two thousand other billionaires in America.

That is why I worry about extreme income inequality. The conditions of the less fortunate must be addressed, but the conditions of the extremely fortunate to have insane amounts of political influence, control media coverage, and influence public perception could end democracy.

Inevitably, someone is going to read this and go, "Aha! Clearly, I can stop reading here because this guy is one of them Marxist Commies." Let me say now, I'm an MBA student. Without getting too technical, that's kind of the opposite of a communist. Also, you're probably using those words wrong, so keep reading.

CLIMATE CRISIS
No drop in an ocean thinks it's responsible for the flood. In the same way, no one wants to consider their own role in a scary-sounding climate crisis. By now, it's no longer a matter of whether or not someone believes in climate change. It's clear that it's real and made significantly worse by human actions. Instead, the issue is whether or not someone understands our impact.

The question is no longer how can we afford climate measures. The question is: How could we afford not to?

---

9   Evers-Hillstrom, "The Price of Victory Is Steep."

Back in the 1980s, America's weather was much less extreme. America suffered three of these extreme events on average per year, which did $17.5 billion of damage on average each year. Not only is the damage increasing each year, but also the rate at which it's increasing is increasing every year. In the last five years, America has had an average of fourteen of these disasters per year. Per year, which has incurred a cost of $107 billion every year. For those of us who aren't math majors, we're spending a little over six times of what we were spending in the '80s just on climate disaster relief every year.[10]

Remember how I said that this is only getting faster? In the last three years, those numbers shot up to fifteen disasters per year that cost $154 billion. In the last three years, our average is almost nine times what we spent in the 1980s. If the trend were only a straight line, we would expect to spend around a trillion dollars per year on disaster relief alone in forty years.

Even if someone doesn't understand the science behind climate change, it's clear that the financial cost of it is real and will continue to get worse. The best-case scenario is that we collectively go bankrupt trying to fight the effects of environmental change. The worst-case scenario is that Earth becomes uninhabitable for human life.

It's immoral to wipe out life as we know it on planet Earth in the cosmic blink of an eye. It's immoral that we are in a man-made extinction event that's happening twenty-five times faster than the average point in Earth's existence.

---

10   Smith, "US Billion-Dollar Weather."

How can we afford not to do anything?

I believe in smart fiscal policy. Sometimes, someone has to be an adult in the room and say, "We can't afford that."

We cannot afford inaction.

HEALTH CARE

"The health and vitality of our people are at least as well worth conserving as their forests, waters, lands, and minerals, and in this great work, the national government must bear a most important part." —Theodore Roosevelt

The state of health care in the United States is frankly embarrassing. Despite the fact that we lead the world in medical innovation, we struggle to provide our citizens with even the most basic level of care. Tens of thousands of Americans die each year because they cannot afford basic care, while half a million people go bankrupt every year due to medical expenses.

Take insulin, for example. About twelve million Americans with diabetes need insulin or will suffer serious consequences and possibly die. This is a medication that they need to take on average about twice a day. However, prices in America are eight times higher than in other developed nations. The average price for insulin is $98.70 in America. Right across the border in Canada, the average price is $12. In the UK, the same vial costs $7.52.[11] Again, this is the same product

---

11   McGrail, "Insulin Prices 8x Higher."

in each country, and it's been on the market since 1982. Yet diabetics are taking to rationing their insulin and are dying when this goes wrong.[12]

Yes, it's a good thing that America is leading the way to develop cures for increasingly niche diseases. However, the fact of the matter is a system that doesn't preclude people from precautionary medicine or allows them to go to doctor visits to keep up with their health would prevent them from life-ruining illnesses down the line. Nearly a quarter of Americans report having skipped basic preventative health care because they simply can't afford it. This can turn into leaving serious conditions undiscovered because people can't afford doctor visits. Additionally, no one should go bankrupt treating their illness just to stay alive.

Tying health care to employment wasn't a great idea before a pandemic, and it certainly wasn't a great idea during a pandemic. COVID-19 simply exposed the flaws in our system. Having fifteen million people lose their jobs and therefore their insurance during a pandemic, the exact time you would want to have health care, made this plain as day. Americans spend more on their health care and get worse results than any other developed country. We can't afford inaction.

Now, what do these three issues have in common?

---

12   Sable-Smith, "Insulin's High Cost."

SUSTAINABLE VALUES

What these issues all have in common is that they are fueled by sustainable values. They're sustainable in two senses:

1. **Sustainable for the health of the country:** Environmental sustainability is pretty self-explanatory. You're not taking from the world around us in a way that leaves it permanently damaged. Managing inequality and health care stewards our system just as environmentalism sustains the planet.

Proponents of capitalism and the American Dream proudly tout how it's possible for even people from humble beginnings to build their own success, but this can easily change. Societies with greater inequality have the least class mobility.[13] If inequality gets out of hand, it'll get harder and harder for people to move between classes, and the American Dream will become even further out of reach.

Access to health care is a large part of this. Between a child who can go to the doctor to stay healthy and one who is always sick because they don't have access to health care, which would you expect to perform better in school? The kid who can go to the doctor, naturally. These effects compound over a lifetime. If the healthy kid outperforms the other due to their health from elementary through high school, that child will have their pick of colleges or trade schools. If that advantage continues, they'll have their pick of careers and will be able to outperform in those roles to increase their compensation. There are myriad inputs that will determine one's success, but

---

13   Hertel and Groh-Samberg, "Relation between Inequality."

health is crucial. "Life, Liberty, and the Pursuit of Happiness" starts with the concept of Life for a reason.

Each of these three values will help us steward our way of life. Health care will allow our citizens to stay alive and achieve their full potential. Reducing inequality will help America to continue to allow citizens a fair shot at success. Environmentalism will allow the planet to continue sustaining human life.

2. **Not the fad of the month:** These values are wellsprings for policy even as opinions about cultural issues change. Trends in culture are part of life, and they are damn near impossible to predict. Life is going to be different in ten, twenty, one hundred years, and we won't know what things will be like. Do you think someone forty years ago could've predicted that we primarily consume our music through streaming or that radio has been replaced by podcasts? Probably not, and that's why I don't think we could predict niche political fads.

Sustainable values, on the other hand, will help us to form policies as the world continues to change. It's a lot like how great parents won't just tell their children what to do but raise them so that they can make smart decisions themselves. Don't tell people what to think but teach them how to think. If someone values social mobility and clean air, it's more likely that I'll trust their decision-making process. The values I've outlined are ones that I think will stay constant even as everything else changes, but yours might be different.

One thing that helps make these values sustainable is that they are positive values rather than negative values. That is to say, these are things that I think should be the case rather than things I think shouldn't be the case. Positive values are stronger values. Societies are better organized around things people do believe in rather than things they don't believe in. There's a reason that the Bill of Rights starts with freedom of speech rather than, for example, it's bad to tell people what they can say.

This is the main reason I think running against Trumpism is doomed to fail in the long run. Politicians are more effective when they say, "this is what I stand for" rather than "this is what I stand against."

It boils down to how the human mind works. Cognitive scientist George Lakoff studies how the brain's makeup influences how we think, saying, "The shape of the brain structures how you understand the world, and any idea you have that you've learned, that you use over and over again that's part of your conceptual system is physically represented in your brain."[14]

We have an organ that gives us all of our ability to think, and this fact influences how we end up thinking. This is so obvious that it's easy to forget.

Here's an example: Say you're at a party, and you strike up a conversation with a stranger. They're fairly charming, and the conversation progresses. Being the social butterfly you are, you ask, "So what do you do?"

"Well, I'm certainly not a pedophile," the charming stranger says.

---

14 *University of California Television* (UCTV), "George Lakoff: Moral Politics."

So, what do you think? The dude's totally a pedophile, right?

Lakoff teaches us that when people hear "Not X," they immediately think of X. The title of his most famous book, Don't Think of an Elephant, reflects this fact.

If your entire platform is based around saying that you are "Not Trumpism," you're broadcasting the word "Trumpism" straight into their brain. Plus, you're not going to convince someone who doesn't already dislike Trumpism. Even when he's long gone, kicking that corpse just ingrains his memory further. We want to believe that people are perfectly rational, but exposure breeds comfort. On a deep level, we're all more comfortable with some pretty hateful shit just because we've been exposed to it for four years. The easiest way to beat this is to simply stop doing it.

Yes, I am aware that I am doing it right now, but just to say, we need to kick the habit.

YOUR VALUES

For you to reflect on your own values, let's look to the title of this chapter for inspiration.

What are the biggest issues facing America?

If you think any of these issues are the absolute biggest threat, are you willing to support policies and politicians to remedy this situation?

For you, the reader, this is a useful question because if you don't take the time for some self-reflection on what your values are, someone else is going to tell them to you. So maybe save that self-reflection until after you've finished reading this book, okay?

CHAPTER 2

SAME TEAM

Bill Maher, for better or worse, is known for speaking his mind. The comedian-turned-political-commentator made his television-hosting debut with the show Politically Incorrect, which aired in 1993 and ran until 2002 when it was canceled in large part due to Maher's habit of controversial remarks. He was given another chance in 2003, when HBO introduced Real Time with Bill Maher, which, as of 2021, is still on the air.

Real Time runs a somewhat standard comedy/commentary blend format, opening with a monologue by Maher, followed by an interview with a guest, a panel discussion featuring commentators from the right and left, and ending with a segment of jokes called "New Rules." After a few minutes of grousing about current events or everyday life ("New Rule: the pizza shops serving the greasiest foods need to stop being the ones that give the tiniest goddamn napkins," is par for the course), he fleshes a one-liner out into a five- or ten-minute rant about the state of the world. Sometimes these can be pretty meh, like when he opined, we need to spend more time shaming the obese into losing weight (I'll pass).

Few people on the Left pride themselves on speaking without a filter, and occasionally this blind squirrel finds an acorn. Having someone on your side of the aisle constantly throwing stuff at the wall to see what sticks will occasionally lead to a good point. The best example of this is Maher's New Rule "Democrats Need a Coach," where he outlines three insightful points (He actually outlines four points, but I'm going to ignore "No More Candidates in the Primary," because the primary is long past.)[15] In order, the points are:

1. Go Where the Votes Are

2. Stand Up to Twitter

3. Message Discipline

When I talk about politics with friends who consider themselves apolitical, I make the comparison between Republicans and the New England Patriots. If all you care about is who wins, you'll become a Patriots fan. Simple as that. Unfortunately, that leaves the Democrats as my beloved Jets, and the only way you can be a Jets fan through the last twenty or fifty years is if winning isn't a huge priority.

The audience for a book on politics may not be into sports but bear with me. I grew up in New Jersey as a Jets fan but spent the last three years living in Boston, the home of the Jets' historical rivals, the Patriots. All you need to know here is that the Jets have been terrible for roughly as long as I've been alive, while the Patriots have been in the Super Bowl

---

15 *Real Time with Bill Maher*, "New Rule: Democrats Need a Coach."

three times in the last five years despite cheating allegations, and their fans are just as loud, proud, and loyal as you might have heard. This just about exhausts my knowledge of football, so I'm going to leave it to your local sports radio channel to debate "deflate-gate" until the end of eternity, as they seem content to do.

On the other hand, we have pretty decisive proof that the GOP is single-mindedly focused on winning. All you need to look at is:

- The continued existence of the electoral college (only one presidential race this millennium has had a Republican win more than 50 percent of the vote).[16]

- Donald Trump coming out against mail-in voting even during a pandemic because "You'd never have a Republican elected in this country again."[17]

- Decades of voter disenfranchisement have culminated with the 2018 and 2020 scandals in Georgia and Wisconsin, respectively.

- Right-wing politicians spreading the conspiracy theory that the 2020 election was rigged despite no proof found by the Supreme Court, Trump's Justice Department, or offers of financial reward for proof.[18],[19]

---

16 Astor, "The Electoral College Is Close."
17 Queally, "Trump Admits."
18 Liptak, "Supreme Court Rejects Republican Challenge."
19 Benner and Schmidt, "Barr Acknowledges No Voter Fraud."

It's part of the GOP culture. If the only thing you care about is winning, you're going to be a fan of the Patriots.

So how do we turn around the Bad News Bears? Let's start with Point 1.

1. GO WHERE THE VOTES ARE

Maher means this in a media sense, as one of his pet projects is getting liberals to go on Fox News, as he told Adam Schiff and many others. Your thoughts on Fox News aside, it's a great point: Fox News has had a nineteen-year streak as the most-watched cable news network, with 3.5 million primetime viewers.[20] As much as progressives paint Fox as a far-right den of propaganda (and it is), it's still the most popular cable news source in the country, which means a fair amount of its viewership is likely to consider itself as politically moderate. Without a chance to hear a liberal's viewpoint on Fox, the average person may not hear them.

Smarter people than I have made the case that Fox is far-right propaganda that normalizes dog-whistle remarks breeds a culture of sexual harassment, and had an incestuous relationship with the Trump White House that bordered on state-run propaganda. But even if that's the case, it behooves liberals to get on the show and get their points out there. Since Tucker Carlson was on Crossfire, his shows have had a liberal on the show to have a semblance of balance, but that wasn't an effort to actually be balanced. That was for good TV. Your points look even better if you have someone

---

20 Flood, "Fox News 19 Straight Years."

in the other seat saying the weakest, watered down versions of liberal talking points.

Letting someone else portray your views runs the risk of having them portrayed in the worst possible way or in bad faith. We've seen that happen since Tucker wore bow ties.

It is shocking that when he was the presidential candidate, Joe Biden appeared once on the nation's largest cable news channel during the election, outside of broadcasted debates. Yes, they don't like him. Yes, they slander him. Yes, going on may inadvertently lead to them being able to point themselves as "fair and balanced" and earn more advertising money. But you can use their platform to deliver your message! At a minimum, three million primetime viewers can hear Democratic talking points! After all, 5.8 million tuned in to watch Trump's interview with Chris Wallace, with countless others seeing clips of the president bragging that he passed a basic cognitive function test. When Bernie Sanders had a town hall meeting on the network in March 2020, he received a standing ovation from the audience.

One key area that Maher doesn't touch on, however, is where to reach people who aren't Fox News viewers. Three and a half million daily viewers are a large number of people, but in a nation of 330 million, that's just over 1 percent of the population. Sure, the fact that the Fox viewership skews older and the elderly are more likely to vote means the audience is more likely to vote. But this forgets the fact that cable news as an industry is not predicted to have a bright future.

Trump frequently brags about how he's got the best ratings, and while this is a pretty stupid thing for a president to brag about, he has a point. He seems to have single-handedly kept the cable news industry alive for at least four more years. Between 2008 and 2014, primetime cable news viewership fell by a third but put up monstrous viewership numbers during his campaign and presidency. And it's hard to see another reason besides Trump.[21] As the ex-CEO of CBS pointed out, Trump "may be bad for America, but he's damn good for CBS."[22]

All of this is to say that there will be more nontraditional mediums (e.g., YouTube and Tik Tok) for conservative news to pop up in, and the Democrats ground game should be focused on getting on these shows, especially as this will pay off huge dividends in the long run. Podcast listeners may be young and unlikely to vote now, but reaching them now will pay off as they get older and more likely to vote. It's not a coincidence that Andrew Yang and Bernie Sanders did so well with younger people, especially after appearing on the Joe Rogan podcast when the average age of his listeners is twenty-four.[23]

As an aside, when I think of undecided voters my own age, I think of Joe Rogan listeners. His podcast, the Joe Rogan Experience, has eight and a half million subscribers on YouTube alone and gets 190 million monthly downloads.[24] Even going off of the YouTube subscribers, he has almost three times the viewership of primetime Fox. While Rogan probably

---

21 Derek Thompson, "Cable News Got Filthy Rich."
22 Collins, "Les Moonves: Trump's Run."
23 "Audience Demographic Variations," *Media Monitors.*
24 Koetsier, "Joe Rogan Takes $100 Million."

wouldn't consider himself a moderate, he likely would consider himself undecided as a voter until shortly before the elections. A running joke is that Rogan's opinion on anything is whatever the last person told him was, and anecdotally a few of the podcast listeners I know have been engaged by both the subtly alt-right personalities on his show and the Sanders and Yang appearances.

When I think of a Joe Rogan listener, I think of someone who likes to hear cool shit and loves to hear cool shit that applies to their life. It makes sense that if more politicians took the time to go on and explain how a green jobs program would help them personally, they would help sway millions of voters. Some on the left think he's a bad guy for having on people like Jordan Peterson or Alex Jones, but it doesn't seem that an audience (which is mostly straight, male, and bro-y) really gives a shit whether people want to cancel him for relatively minor reasons. He's not going anywhere, so use it to help out.

Figuring out where the next big conservative station will be is as difficult to figure out as wherever the hell Tomi Lahren is these days, but there's got to be some intern at the DNC with an ear to the ground. Suck it up and go dunk on Ben Shapiro with your own facts and logic. Sure, Stephen Crowder is annoying, but he's only able to debate college freshmen, so you'll look great. And for God's sake, someone figures out what's going on with Charlie Kirk's shrunken face.

2. STAND UP TO TWITTER

A successful team should be able to view the game footage and see what worked well for the other team.

One of the most effective tools in Donald Trump's kit was that he made it a point to never apologize, no matter how badly he fucked up. When he finally declared a national emergency due to coronavirus, his exact words about how things had gotten to that point were, "I take no responsibility."[25] These are the words of a narcissist who probably genuinely believed that he did nothing wrong, but his supporters respond well to this kind of thing.

The only real recorded apology I could find Trump making was for his Access Hollywood tape, where he bragged to Billy Bush about sexually assaulting women. The Trump campaign released two videos in response, and in the first video, he said, "I apologize if anyone was offended." The next video actually showed him apologizing, but it quickly turned from an apology to saying, "Bill Clinton has actually abused women, and Hillary has bullied, attacked, shamed, and intimidated his victims. We will discuss this more in the coming days. See you at the debate on Sunday."[26] When Sunday rolled around, he gave front-row seats to multiple women who had accused Bill Clinton of assault or harassment, and the media coverage shifted to that fact.[27] (I'm going to take a hard stance here and say that sexual assault is bad, and anyone who rapes people shouldn't be president. I'm using this example because it's literally the most substantive apology of his I could find.)

This episode exemplifies the Donald Trump Media Scandal Response. Usually, they don't start with an apology. The

---

25   Smith, "'I Don't Take Responsibility.'"
26   Farley, "Trump's Rare Apology."
27   Nuzzi, "Donald Trump Brings Four Accusers."

tone is one of "I didn't do it, but if someone did do it, one of my political enemies did it worse." He then does something outlandish to start a new media cycle.

His refusal to apologize is one of the reasons his supporters viewed him as "strong." Whether they thought he was wrongly persecuted or whether they didn't care if he had done it, this is one of the keys to his success. If you don't like what people are saying, change the conversation.

It's very dangerous when the most powerful man on the planet is literally unable to conceive of the fact that he did wrong, especially when it's something like how his lack of action led to the deaths of half a million people due to a pandemic. Sometimes people really do fuck up in inexcusable ways, like a decades-long trail of harassment and abuse, and these merit action to fix that fact. But that's not what most of these issues boil down to.

On a subconscious level, most people do want to feel like they're being led by a strong leader. The left lets itself get bogged down by apologizing for things that don't affect most people's lives. As Bill Maher said during the Democratic primary, "I think I know more about what people have apologized for than their stances on the issues."[28] When you get sucked into that news cycle, it takes the media coverage out of the good things you plan on doing for people.

Democrats need to stop focusing on why people shouldn't hate them and talk about why people should love them.

---

28 *Real Time with Bill Maher*, "New Rule: Democrats Need a Coach."

The sort of person that's going to shit on you for small-time identity issues isn't going to magically become the sort of person who loves you. Outrage is a game, and people get too much enjoyment out of it. When one of the biggest talking points outside of the party is that the culture warriors want to cancel everything, you don't earn points by willingly putting your own neck on the chopping block unnecessarily.

3. MESSAGE DISCIPLINE

The Dolphins don't do it. The Devils don't do it. Bundesliga doesn't do it.

Why are Democrats the only team that sees game footage of the opposition working in sync and says, "Well, how goddamn dare they"?

For all the faults of the Patriots, every position on the team has a role. Andrews snaps to Brady, Brady throws to Welker, Welker runs it in for six. Rinse. Repeat. Sports analogies are trite but accurate.

Republicans work as a team as well. In their media appearances, Republicans are very skilled at hitting the same talking points and using the same words, to the point that MSNBC has played montages of Republicans using the exact same phrases. The Trump 2020 campaign even launched a website called "snowflakevictory.com" filled with Republican talking points for voters to talk about issues over the holiday season, headlined "How to Win an Argument with Your Liberal Relatives."[29] In

---

29 *MSNBC*, "Trump Campaign Gives Talking Points."

short, they "all get in a room and get a talking point that they all say," as Maher pointed out.[30]

This isn't a weakness. This dedication to message discipline is one of the strongest tools they have.

George Lakoff has a great explanation:

> "Back in the 1950s, conservatives hated each other. The financial conservatives hated the social conservatives. The libertarians did not get along with the social conservatives or the religious conservatives. And many social conservatives were not religious. A group of conservative leaders got together around William F. Buckley Jr. and others and started asking what the different groups of conservatives had in common and whether they could agree to disagree in order to promote a general conservative cause. They started magazines and think tanks and invested billions of dollars. . . . Every Wednesday, Grover Norquist has a group meeting—around eighty people—of leaders from the full range of the right. They

---

30 *Real Time with Bill Maher*, "New Rule: Democrats Need a Coach."

are invited, and they debate. They work out their differences, agree to disagree, and when they disagree, they trade-off. The idea is, this week, he'll win on his issue. Next week, I'll win on mine. Each one may not get everything he wants, but over the long haul, he gets a lot of what he wants."[31] (emphasis mine)

Rand Paul might bitch and moan as a libertarian who wants to cut all government spending, but when it's time to roll over and increase the Pentagon budget by a hundred billion dollars, he's there. Why? Because Republicans are in lockstep here.

Lakoff outlines six types of progressives:

- Socioeconomic progressives who think everything can be boiled down to money and class

- Identity politics progressives

- Environmentalists

- Civil liberties progressives

- Spiritual progressives

- Antiauthoritarians[32]

---

31 Lakoff, *The ALL NEW Don't Think of an Elephant!* 13-15.
32 Ibid.

Obviously, there will be overlap, and people can be multiple of these at the same time, but it's a useful outline.

We haven't learned the lesson that we're all on the same team, and you can make compromises within the party. Part of this is due to the fact that party leaders see the rise of populist progressives as a threat to their control and try to limit their sway. It's like an aging captain lashing out at the new superstar because no one is buying the former's jersey anymore. Entrenched power has led to some major whiffs on policy, such as failing to adopt legalized marijuana into the DNC platform by a one hundred and five to sixty vote, despite the fact that 66 percent of Americans support it.[33] But in the short term, they need to all get in a room and agree on a talking point and then say it.

Longer-term, the left needs to address its media incompetency. The right has had a long head start by throwing huge amounts of money at think tanks to spit out cause-friendly research (in 2002, the right spent four times as much money on research in think tanks and had four times as much media time, for example).[34] The right is also more willing to spend money on media that may not turn a profit in the short term because the long-term benefits are enormous. Ben Shapiro, for example, received seed funding from fracking billionaires and now creates content that is consistently in the top ten most shared links on Facebook almost every day.[35, 36] Turn-

---

33 Halaschak, "AOC: Marijuana Legalization."
34 Lakoff, "George Lakoff's 'Framing 101.'"
35 "Ben Shapiro 'Owns the Libs'...But Who Owns Him?" *TYT*.
36 Facebook's Top 10 (@FacebooksTop10), Twitter.

ing Point USA is funded in part by the Koch brothers, and while their finances aren't public, I'd be shocked if they were turning a profit.[37] Right-wing billionaires are content with writing blank checks to these companies because they stand to gain tens of millions of dollars of value from it.

There are no longer walls between what is "serious" messaging and what is frivolous. Funny, memetic messaging will act as a Trojan Horse for your message, or it can shoot you in the foot, as Hillary Clinton showed us all when she told us to "Pokémon GO to the polls!" Meanwhile, every time I hear Ted Cruz, my brain automatically says "Lyin' Ted" because it just works. The media literate younger generation needs to be treated like they know what they're doing, like when Alexandria Ocasio-Cortez led a class on social media presence one of her first days in Congress. Funny, savvy people get away with more. Lean into it.

The only thing that can stop a bad guy who makes great TV is a good guy who makes great TV.

At the end of the day, if you want to win, you have to play like a team. Go to your audience and then grow your audience. Show them that you have the self-respect to stand up and focus on your winning ideas. Have every member play their part, and don't put the star players out in the cold.

After all, "winning is a habit, but so is losing."[38]

---

37   Kotch, "Koch Foundation Criticizes Turning Point."
38   *Real Time with Bill Maher*, "New Rule: Democrats Need a Coach."

CHAPTER 3

STRATEGIC INITIATIVES: PLAYING THE LONG GAME

Here's one reason that Republicans are able to win elections: more strategic initiatives.

What does that mean? They have a big picture goal and then little goals that help them reach the big picture goal. Basically, the sum is greater than its parts because the parts feed into each other and support each other.

Think for a second about what the Republican party ran on during the Reagan years, for example: lower taxes, because they don't trust the government. Lowering taxes for the Republicans is the supreme strategic initiative because it creates a vicious cycle. Republicans don't want people to trust the government; therefore, you should give the government less money. If the government has less money to function, then it doesn't work. A government that doesn't work isn't trustworthy. Therefore, we should pay it less taxes.

George Lakoff defines strategic initiatives as "a plan in which a change in one carefully chosen issue area has automatic effects over many, many, many other issue areas."[39]

I don't fault the Republicans for having strategic initiatives any more than I fault Bill Belichick for turning the Patriots into a power-house team: It's making the world a worse place, but it's their job, and they're fucking good at it.

What strategic initiatives do Democrats have? No, seriously. This is an open-ended question because I don't think they have a team strategy here. Sure, they have a lot of independent issues that they collectively care about, but they don't form a collective vision. If you can't explain your plan in thirty seconds, you might not have the master plan you think you do.

It makes you wish that Democrats were anywhere near as cool and crafty as Fox makes them out to be. Sometimes in the gym, I would overhear Tucker Carlson telling the world how Democrats were using the BLM movement to instill radical Marxism and somehow end climate change in the process. God, I wish! Instead, we're stuck with a party that couldn't negotiate for a $5 sandwich at Subway. Sometimes, when I can't sleep, I'll turn on Fox to hear about how Biden is forcing every child to seize the wealth of billionaires and sigh longingly.

---

39 Lakoff, *The ALL NEW Don't Think of an Elephant!*, 26.

WHAT WOULD A DEMOCRATIC STRATEGIC INITIATIVE LOOK LIKE?

Let's reflect on the problems we've discussed:

- Wealth inequality is skyrocketing. The ultrarich are getting richer, which allows them to seize more power.

- An ultrawealthy class will become more powerful than the government but also encourage us to further weaken the government.

- Working people are earning less money every year as wages stagnate.

- A poorer working class has less of a say in our government. (More money gives you a bigger microphone, and we had a Supreme Court ruling saying that money equals speech in Citizens United.)

- Climate change leads to more extreme weather, which will disproportionately affect the poor. It's like Ted Cruz leaving Texas for Cancun during the blizzard, except we're the ones stuck without power.

- People don't believe that the government works for them because it's controlled by the wealthy.

- Only one party is running on the idea that the system is rigged against average people and promising to fix it, but only uses Band-Aids.

A Democratic Strategic Initiative might aim to reduce inequality by empowering working-class people with higher pay and more equal treatment and in the process, show people that the government works for them. Maybe this would look like a public investment program to pay people living wages and put pressure on employers to match those living wages. The goal of this public investment program could be to combat an issue that will affect every single human being so that everyone has a vested interest in seeing it succeed. This program could be financed by taxing wealth that people think was generated at their expense to create support for it.

Not only would this help people materially, but it would remind people that the government works on their behalf. Tell people that you're going to help them and then do it, so the next time you say you have their best interests at heart, they believe you. Later on in the book, I'll examine the smaller initiatives, but for the rest of this chapter, I'm going to write about the big picture mindset we should aim to change.

REMIND PEOPLE WHY WE HAVE A GOVERNMENT

This February, Tim Cadogan, the CEO of GoFundMe, published an op-ed titled "Hello Congress, Americans Need Help and We Can't Do Your Job for You."[40] GoFundMe is a crowdsourced fundraising website where people say, "I would like to raise money for X" reason and then strangers help contribute. It's helped a lot of people.

---

40 Cadogan, "GoFundMe CEO: Hello Congress."

What's terrifying is that the CEO of the company had to write a piece about how people are over-relying on his platform. Between March and August, they had over 150,000 campaigns for COVID-related financial assistance on their page. GoFundMe is powerful, but it's not designed to replace the functioning of the government, which should support its people in a time of need.

We have a government for a reason, and it needs to function in a way that will restore faith in it.

Reagan's legacy is dragging us down from beyond the grave. I don't mean selling guns to Iran to destabilize South America. I don't mean having a television star who is experiencing dementia run for president and winning just because a lot of Americans thought he seemed nice and looked past the fact that he's a terrible person.

Reagan poisoned the well by declaring that "Government IS the problem." People had misgivings about the government before, but the impact of having the head of the government saying this was huge. It's like having a professor come in and say, "I am waaaaay too drunk to teach this class right now;" students may have had some complaints, but it created serious credibility issues in the long run. This idea was then adopted into mainstream politics, and after hearing this message for forty years, Americans are willing to roll over for corporate overlords and thank them for the opportunity to be stepped on.

The fact of the matter is that there are some things a government is uniquely suited to do and many things that corporations can't do. Simply put, the government protects our freedoms. No one gives us our freedoms. We are born with them. However, these freedoms need to be protected, and the only body that can do that is the collective rule of the people, otherwise known as our government. Corporations can make some excellent products, but they can't protect our human rights.

Trump being banned from Twitter and Facebook opened up a discussion on the right about free speech and the power of corporations that we've been ignoring for years. Personally, I think it's really funny that the same people who screech about free markets were freaking out that the free market decided insurrections are bad for business and banned people from planning them on their platforms. But, if this is what it takes to have people acknowledge that corporations may have too much power, I'll take it.

Facebook isn't here to protect your freedom of speech. Facebook is here to make as much money as possible by using your personal data. Instead:

THE GOVERNMENT IS OUR CONTRACT TO PROTECT OUR FREEDOMS
"The government is like a lawyer who represents all of us. . . . It's time for the advocate for all of us to actually fight on our behalf."
—ANAND GIRIDHARADAS[41]

---

41 *The Daily Show with Trevor Noah*, "Anand Giridharadas-Winners Take All."

You can think about freedom in two forms: Freedoms To and Freedoms From.[42] Freedoms To gets all of the attention, but if we're not careful, we will lose our Freedoms From. For example, Americans have the Freedom To own certain firearms. Because our government fails to act, however, we have lost our Freedom From the fear of school shootings. This isn't a new idea. Philosophy nerds sometimes call them "Positive and Negative Freedoms," but it's the same concept.

Both are important, but the recent trend is toward the power of Freedoms To to trample over our Freedoms From.

The most pressing example of this in our current society is the over-reliance on corporations and the free market to solve our problems. It's a fine idea on paper, but it's clear that a fanatical devotion toward deregulation is crippling our country. After forty-plus years of propaganda, people believe that unregulated markets are the solution to all of life's problems, and suggesting otherwise will label you a communist.

But here's a secret: the market is run by humans, and humans are (last I checked) fallible. Humans do shitty things and make mistakes; therefore, the market does shitty things and makes mistakes.

Free enterprise is a powerful thing, but our corporations believe it's their duty to make the most amount of money for the people who own them. Corporations are profit-maximizing machines. You can't leave it up to them to act responsibly on their own because it's simply not in their charter. Birds chirp, dogs bark, and corporations make as much money as they can. It's just what they do.

---

42 Carter, "Positive and Negative Liberty."

Corporations and the wealthy are going to try and convince you that paying their taxes or paying employees a living wage will force them to shutter their doors and the CEO to sell his beach house. That's because they are profit-maximizing machines. It's cheaper to convince you that you should be paid less than it is for them to pay you. It's cheaper to convince you that they can't afford to pay taxes than it is to pay their taxes. It's cheaper to pollute than it is to keep the air clean. The next time someone tries to convince you otherwise, please keep the profit-driven machines in the back of your mind.

Powerful people will tell you that you can't tell them what to do, but the end result of this is that you will be less able to live your life as you please. We need our collective lawyer to protect our freedom.

WITHOUT YOUR FREEDOM FROMS, YOU HAVE NO FREEDOMS TO
Would you take a few million dollars in exchange for a six-months-to-live cancer diagnosis? Probably not. Now imagine that the choice was made for you: You wouldn't have the Freedom To live your natural life.

This might seem like an oversimplification, but this is the reality of the situation for many people. Bayer-Monsanto has been sued thousands of times for selling products that contain ingredients that cause cancer. The most famous of these cases came in 2019 when they were successfully sued for $75 million for giving one man non-Hodgkin's lymphoma.[43]

---

43   Zaveri, "Monsanto Weedkiller Roundup."

I'm willing to bet here that Monsanto made a whole lot more than $75 million in profit from the sale of Roundup, which means paying off a dying man was just a cost of doing business for them to reach greater profits. Without the government, our collective lawyer, outlawing carcinogens and punishing those who break the law, Monsanto and every other corporation will continue to ruin lives as long as it makes them more money than it costs them. Your Freedoms From are being stepped on.

- You have a Freedom From your weed killers giving you cancer.

- You should have a Freedom From your bank making money off you going broke through overdraft fees and other predatory practices.

- You should have a Freedom From the planet heating up until it's unlivable.

Without being Free From these issues, you won't be Free To pursue a fulfilling life. Someone with hundreds of thousands of dollars of student loan debt isn't really free to start a family, or buy a house, or choose a fulfilling job that won't pay off their debt in this lifetime. Maybe this is why Millennials aren't starting families, buying houses, or starting their own businesses.[44, 45, 46]

---

44 Barroso, Parker and Jesse Bennett, "How Millennials Approach Family Life."
45 Fry, "Living With Parents."
46 Wilkinson, "Why Millennials Aren't Starting Businesses."

We like to imagine that freedom comes to all people equally and all at once, but there are many types of freedoms, and they affect people differently. If the sort of freedoms we prioritize are giving the wealthy and powerful carte blanche to do whatever they want, everyone else gets pushed out of the public sphere and priced out of living a good life.

PRIVATE DEPENDS ON THE PUBLIC

The good things we have are due to a collective effort.

George Lakoff made the point that public works projects like highways used to have signs that said, "Your tax dollars at work!"[47] But they no longer appear, and people have short memories, so they forget about the benefits they reap from paying their dues in society.

Taxes are both your dues to help run the society you benefit from and your investment in its future. Paying them is both the right thing to do and the smart thing to do. You couldn't build that highway by yourself, so you pitch in with the rest of your community and boom, road. It's like a nationwide GoFundMe that you can democratically decide how it gets spent. Neat!

Individuals may do great things, but they wouldn't be able to do so without the infrastructure that we've built. It's like how LeBron James is the greatest basketball player in the game right now, but if the NBA didn't exist, his basketball skills would be useless. The same is true for developments in

---

47   Lakoff, 51.

society. Steve Jobs may get credit for the iPhone, but much of the underlying technology was developed with public funding. The internet, for example, was developed by the US Military, which is why its original name was Arpanet.[48] The University of Hawai'i needed a new way to wire its campus despite the islands' complicated geography, so they created a wireless internet service called Alohanet, which gave rise to mobile, satellite, cellular, and Wi-Fi communications.[49] Multi-touch technology was developed by a University of Delaware graduate student before it was sold to Apple.[50] Even private research universities like Stanford (where Google was developed by graduate students) receive millions in federal government funding. If you want to go really broad, providing basic education to all children provides the infrastructure for millions of young minds to either develop these technologies or work at the companies that will put them to use. Hell, building a nationwide highway system makes it possible for goods to get from the factory to the stores where people buy them.

To be clear, technology transfer, or "transferring the right to commercialize innovations that result from scientific research . . . to corporate entities that can make them into marketable products that can be made available to the public, and ultimately, improve people's lives," is, for the most part, a good thing.[51] My iPhone is an incredibly useful tool, and I'm glad some designers in California can make such a sexy tool to help me find a doughnut shop that's open at 9 p.m. in a town I've never been to.

---

48   Zimmermann, "Internet History Timeline."
49   Arakaki, "Pioneering Wireless Technology."
50   Roberts, "UD Inventors of Touch Imaging."
51   Ibid.

But these things would've never come about without public investment, and America needs to be reminded of that fact. I'm proud that my small contribution of taxes goes toward developing impressive technology that makes all of our lives easier. The government has the funding to help researchers develop technology that might not turn a profit for years, and that's a good thing. We will all benefit from it in the long run. The private depends upon the public.

FEED THE BEAST

Funding the government is a long-term investment in our future, and it's a winning strategy. Unfortunately, while the Republican strategy has been to defund the government and tell people it doesn't work, the Democrats haven't come up with a winning rebuttal.

The long-term strategy should be to show that we have a government to do something no other institution can do and that you should be proud to be a part of it. Sure, it's an imperfect force, but it's the only force we have powerful enough to stand up against the alternative. Paying your taxes is patriotic. Stop apologizing.

Giving the government the resources it needs to function enables the rest of us to go about our daily lives. Sometimes these generate insane returns. Every dollar invested in NASA, for example gives between a 700 percent to 4,000 percent return.[52] (Talk about investments mooning.)

---

52 McKay, McKay, and Duke, "NASA Scientific and Technical Information."

We are going up against forty years of some of the most deep-seated propaganda in human history. How do you convince people that the government is by them and for them? Simple: Provide some policies that actually help everyday people and then hype the hell out of them.

What kind of policies would work here? Glad you asked—let's start with the next chapter. Turn the page, and let's begin.

CHAPTER 4

MAULED BY BLUE CROSS

Allena Hansen was working in her backyard one summer afternoon when she made the terrible mistake of getting attacked by a bear.

While the bear was in the middle of the mauling process, Hansen thrust her thumb into its eyes, which distracted the bear just long enough for her to call to her mastiff and Irish wolfhound. Half blinded, she made it to her car, laughed at her own reflection of one eyeball hanging by a thread out of her skull, and made her way to a fire station. From there, she was airlifted to the UCLA Medical Center.

"That was the easy part," Hansen said.[53]

Unfortunately, after the relatively lighthearted affair of having her face torn off by a black bear, Hansen had to undergo the

---

53 Zoellner, "Woman after Bear Attack."

trauma of dealing with Blue Cross Blue Shield, her health insurance provider of thirty years. You see, having fourteen teeth, an eyeball, and a nose torn out of place only required elective surgery for her to go about her life.

Outside of her monthly premiums and a deductible that resets yearly (long reconstructions take time), Hansen spent an additional $300,000 for surgeries. Plus more than $600 a month in prescription eyedrops, now that she doesn't have tear ducts.

That $300,000 would've gone much higher had Hansen not gone on to "prostitute" herself by becoming the "freak of the week" on television until several doctors took pity on her. One of the donated services was a bridge put in to replace fourteen teeth, which would have cost around $40,000 had she had to pay out of pocket.

Even with all of the assistance provided by good Samaritans, the cost of care "went through all of my retirement savings, my IRAs, my assets. I am now living on a social security pension. Period," she said.[54]

Some people say that the American health care system is the best in the world due to the amount of medical innovation we produce. But was the woman who got her face eaten by a bear lucky that her face was eaten in America rather than, say, Canada?

---

54   Ibid.

WHAT IS MEDICARE FOR ALL?
Let's define some things upfront. Medicare, as it currently exists, is a government health insurance program for people over sixty-five and some people with disabilities. Medicare covers hospital insurance and medical insurance, and then Medicare Advantage covers prescription drug coverage.[55]

"Medicare for All" means everyone has access to the system, not just the elderly. The most popular version of the idea, as championed by Bernie Sanders, would cover all essential treatment while cutting out the premiums or deductibles. Rather than giving your money to insurance companies who may or may not pay for your care, your taxes just go straight toward getting care.

Medicare for All is a single-payer system. Currently, we have a bunch of different insurance companies. If you have Blue Cross Blue Shield insurance like our friend who was attacked by a bear, for example, Aetna pays for your medical care. If you don't have insurance, you pay for your care out of your own pocket. Single-payer would simplify this by only having one payer in the entire market. Some countries that have single-payer systems are Canada, Great Britain, and Sweden.

Single-payer systems eliminate insurance networks. Many doctors only accept one form of insurance or another. Anything that's "out of network" will have to be paid by the patient out of pocket despite the fact that they pay for health insurance. I've personally spent too many hours on my insurance company's website trying to find a doctor who

---

[55] "What's Medicare?" Medicare.gov.

will accept payment from my insurance company because they were in-network. With a single-payer system, everyone takes their payment. Rather than struggling to find someone who can run your bloodwork without costing an arm and a leg, you just go.

Single-payer systems also have skin in the game when it comes to keeping you healthy. Insurance companies make money by getting more people on their system, paying higher rates, and then trying to pay as little as possible. On the other hand, a single-payer system incentivizes preventative care. An insurance company can try to weasel out of paying for your open-heart surgery, but a single-payer will have to pay one way or another. It would rather you just go to the doctor before your condition gets out of hand.

Finally, Bernie's version of Medicare for All would allow the government program to negotiate prescription prices. If those prices are too expensive, pharmacists would be allowed to import drugs from countries where they are cheaper, like Canada. Prices would then be pegged to the prices other wealthy nations like Canada, Germany, and Japan pay.[56] This is important because drug prices in America are currently three times higher than in those countries.[57]

Before we move on, ask yourself—do you love your insurance company that much?

---

56 Ibid.
57 Dunleavy, "RAND."

LESSONS FROM COVID

The natural time for change is when things go wrong. Sure, you hope you can get them correct right out of the gate, but sometimes life doesn't pan out that way. The Constitution was ratified after the Articles of Confederation were shown to be too weak to handle uprisings like Shay's Rebellion.[58] Major Wall Street reforms like the Glass-Steagall Act came after the 1929 Crash.[59] Everybody stopped talking about Game of Thrones when the final season was so bad it wiped the show from public consciousness.

I'm sure that you've heard America spends twice as much money per person on health care than any other developed country.[60] I'm sure that you've heard that we spend anywhere from twice to eight times as much on administration as any other developed country.[61] I'd even bet you know that American life expectancy dropped every year for three years from 2014 to 2017 before shaving off almost 550 days of life expectancy in the first half of the pandemic alone.[62]

But how badly did things go during the pandemic?

According to the Bureau of Labor Statistics, twenty-two million jobs were lost between February and April 2020 due to COVID-19. In November, this eventually stabilized to ten million jobs lost due to the pandemic, the most recent month

---

58 "Shays's Rebellion," Khan Academy.
59 Kenton, "Should We Bring Back Glass-Steagall?"
60 Feldscher, "US Pays More for Health Care."
61 Ibid.
62 Winsor, "US Life Expectancy."

for which the data as of this writing.[63] For comparison, twice as many people lost their jobs in March and April alone as did during the Great Recession.

About 61percent of these people got their coverage from their jobs (called Employer-Sponsored Insurance, or ESI). But Employer-Sponsored Insurance doesn't just cover the employees but also their families and children. One estimate claimed that twenty-seven million people lost their health insurance due to this job loss.[64] Seven million of those people were children. Before the pandemic, eighty-seven million people either didn't have insurance or were underinsured.[65]

Sure, about half of these people may be eligible to get coverage under the Affordable Care Act, and others might be able to get on COBRA (Continuation of Health Coverage plan, essentially continued employer insurance after you lose your job) before Biden's recovery plan fully subsidized COBRA. But these programs aren't exactly cheap. COBRA costs $7,188 for a single person on average and $20,756 for a family. Personally, I find it hard to imagine that many recently unemployed people are going to be able to afford the $20,000 for an entire year to keep their insurance. Additionally, it seems a little silly to have the government subsidize a more expensive form of insurance when a government plan already exists. It's like if you asked to carpool with a friend across the state and they offer to pay for your train ticket instead, you still get where you need to go, but that's not more efficient for anyone.

---

63 "Employment Recovery in the Wake," US Bureau of Labor Statistics.
64 Garfield, Claxton, and Damico, "Eligibility for ACA Coverage."
65 "Health Care Is a Human Right," Elizabeth Warren.

(The estimate of how many employees lost their health insurance seemed low to me, as thirty-one million people applied for unemployment insurance in March and April alone.[66] One study points to the fact that "lower-wage workers are less likely to be covered by their employer's plan and similarly, job losses have been highest and most sustained among industries that tend to have lower coverage rates, e.g., retail, service, hospitality."[67] So, the types of people who lost their jobs were more likely to be underpaid and lack insurance. Hooray?)

It's almost impossible to imagine that this pandemic wasn't exacerbated by people's lack of access to health care. Even before COVID, 22 percent of people reported avoiding basic medical care like doctor's visits or bloodwork due to cost. Fifteen percent of people had had a family member "forgo medical care because it was too expensive."[68] Surely millions of people losing their health insurance would prevent them from getting tested regularly, which would, in turn, keep them from knowing they should quarantine. It would also price them out of being able to get the care they need while they were sick. Preventative care is much cheaper for individuals and society than is care for someone who's already sick.

Data doesn't exist for the number of bankruptcies that came about because of COVID treatment. For those without insurance in need of serious COVID treatment, hospital care averaged around $50,000 for people in their twenties and thirties

---

66 Garfield, Claxton, and Damico, "Eligibility for ACA Coverage."
67 Daniel McDermott et. al, "Pandemic Affected Health Coverage."
68 Megan Leonhardt, "Nearly 1 in 4 Americans."

and nearly $80,000 for those in their forties and fifties.[69] Some of the people who lost their insurance qualified for coverage from the Affordable Care Act or even Medicare coverage—and that's excellent! I wish more people were that lucky. Had we had Medicare for All from the get-go, we would've saved untold human suffering and what will sure to be a wave of medical bankruptcies due to COVID in the near future.

But surely those insane costs are just from a once-in-a-lifetime pandemic. How would Medicare for All save us money in normal times?

IT'S THE FINANCIALS, STUPID

The health care industry has a bit of a spending problem in the same way that Harvey Weinstein's office had a bit of a harassment problem.

Time for some fiscal responsibility. We need to cut spending on this wasteful industry and put this money back in the pockets of the people. (Wow, no one on the left ever gets to say that. What a rush!)

Let's put aside for a moment the fact that American health care performs poorly by several key metrics, like how we have a higher child mortality rate and a lower overall life expectancy than Cuba.[70] Outside of the huge cost of human life, it's also crippling the nation financially.

---

69 Hackett, "Average Cost of Hospital Care."
70 "Cuba vs. United States," *Nationmaster*.

Medicare for All catches a lot of flack for its sticker price, which is indeed pretty large. But what opponents of the act fail to mention is how much money we waste on our current system now. People hear that Medicare for All would cost $3 trillion a year and think, "Wow! That's a lot of money!" and then miss out on the fact that we're currently spending $3.5 trillion a year.[71] We're paying an extra half a trillion a year for worse results!

Alison Galvani, director of Yale's Center for Infectious Disease Modeling and Analysis, released a study last year titled "Improving the Prognosis of Health Care in the United States." Galvani and her team analyzed our system's current costs, estimated how much more it would cost to get everyone covered on Medicare for All, and then subtracted how much money we would save under the system.[72]

The result is that Medicare for All would cut costs by 13 percent, or $450 billion.[73]

Where does the cost cutting come from?

Initially, $219 billion in savings would come from cutting "administrative overhead." It turns out cutting out the middleman can save you a fair amount of money, especially when you account for the fact that "the CEOs of seventy of the largest US health care companies earned $9.8 billion" in the seven years following the passing of the Affordable

---

71 "American Health Care," Committee for a Responsible Federal Budget.
72 Galvani et al., "Improving the Prognosis of Health Care."
73 Ibid.

Care Act.[74] Rather than having dozens of highly paid insurance executives, we would be one administrator making a government salary. Americans would also stop paying for redundant employees at myriad insurance companies. This is equivalent to saving NASA's entire 2020 budget ten times over every single year.[75]

The next largest savings would come from allowing Medicare to negotiate the prices of pharmaceutical drugs. Currently, the federal government isn't allowed to negotiate these rates, which is a large part of the reason drugs are so expensive. Allowing Medicare to negotiate on our collective behalf would save $180 billion per year under Galvani's model.[76] Where our system truly fails us in a preventable way is how much basic medicines are price gouged. Insulin, for example, has been around for one hundred years, but brand-name insulin has skyrocketed in cost 1,200 percent since the 1990s. The drug behind EpiPens, the drug that prevents people with severe allergies from dying of exposure to peanuts or other allergens, has also been around for over a century. In 2016 alone, the price of EpiPens skyrocketed by 400 percent.[77] (Funnily enough, the CEO of the company behind EpiPens is the daughter of Senator Joe Manchin. I'm sure this has nothing to do with his opposition to Medicare for All).

---

74 Herman, "The Sky-High Pay of Health Care CEOs."
75 NASA, "FY 2020 Spending Plan."
76 Galvani et al., "Improving the Prognosis of Health Care in the USA."
77 "Reducing Health Care Costs in America," Elizabeth Warren Campaign.

Another $100 billion in savings comes from applying the lower Medicare fee structure to the rest of the health care industry. Due to the size of the pool of insured people under Medicare, they are able to lower costs for some treatments. One surprising figure comes from the fact that hospitals spend $35 billion trying to track down payments for unpaid bills, which would be eliminated.[78]

The fact that we'd all save money under a single-payer system is pretty intuitive. All insurance companies really are is a middleman between you and the care you need. Removing the middleman just gets rid of an unnecessary cost.

Think of insurance companies like Ticketmaster. When you want to go see a concert, it makes sense that you pay the band for performing and the venue for hosting. If life were simple, you could go to the band's or the venue's website, you'd buy a ticket, and they would send it to you in an email. Instead, Ticketmaster inserts itself in between you and the service you're paying for. You have no real way to get around them, but you promised your cousin Bruce Springsteen tickets, so you have to pay them. Because they know you don't have another option, they jack up the prices by charging you a processing fee, charging you a service fee, and charging you a fee for the privilege of having your tickets emailed rather than mailed. Next thing you know, you're not paying the sticker price just because someone inserted themselves in between you and the Boss. Except in this example, there would be a significant chance that your tickets don't work because the venue is out of network.

---

78   Galvani et al., "Improving the Prognosis of Health Care in the USA."

Now consider the other gains to the economy. Even if you don't give a shit about whether people live or die, if you're an employer, you would prefer your employees would be healthy so they can be more productive. One estimate says that "illness-related lost productivity costs [employers] another $530 billion per year," which "amounts to 60 cents for every dollar employers spend on health care benefits." Not only would employers get the advantage of not having to pay for benefits, but they would also reap the gains of increased productivity.[79]

US employers paid nearly $880 billion in health care benefits for employees and dependents in 2018. However, illness-related lost productivity costs them another $530 billion per year, per a new report from the Integrated Benefits Institute (IBI), a nonprofit health and productivity research organization. That amounts to 60 cents for every dollar employers spend on health care benefits.[80]

Furthermore, picture what people would do if they weren't crippled by medical expenses. Our friend Allena Hansen was out over $300,000. The median income in America is about $65,000, according to the census.[81] Let's say that if she made the median income in America and took home half of that after taxes and living expenses, she'd have to spend ten years giving every extra dollar she earned to pay off her medical debt . . . and she'd still have to pay for her health insurance. What would she do if she didn't have to give every last cent

---

79 "Poor Health Costs US Employers $530 Billion," Integrated Benefits Institute.

80 Ibid.

81 "2019 Median Household Income in the United States," US Census Bureau.

away? Well, she'd probably live like you or I would. She'd go out to eat, or go see a movie, or buy gifts for her nieces or nephews. Maybe save for retirement so she can live her final years with dignity. All of this is to say that she would live a good life and put her money back into the economy. The insurance industry doesn't create wealth; it sucks money away from people like you and me and Allena.

On the off chance you do care about the lives of other human beings, Galvani's study at Yale estimates we would save 68,000 people's lives every year.[82]

MEDICARE FIGHTS INEQUALITY
Imagine you could wave a magic wand that would stop people from going bankrupt—not to prevent them from doing so but eliminating the root cause of why they go bankrupt. That magic wand would look a lot like Medicare for All.

A shocking two-thirds of bankruptcies are caused by medical debt. Before COVID-19, more than half a million people per year (approximately 530,000) declared bankruptcy due to medical debt.[83] Data doesn't exist on how many people went bankrupt due to COVID-19 medical treatment, but I'm willing to bet it's a lot more.

A 2009 Harvard Medical School study found that "nearly 45,000 annual deaths are associated with a lack of health

---

82   Galvani et al., "Improving the Prognosis of Health Care in the USA."
83   Konish, "This Is the Real Reason Most Americans File for Bankruptcy."

insurance."[84] Since 2009, "average family premiums have increased 54 percent, and workers' contribution has increased 71 percent, several times more quickly than wages (26 percent) and inflation (20 percent)."[85] Tens of thousands of people die every year because they can't afford health care, and it's only grown more unaffordable. Not only do the wealthy have access to better care, but the dream of good health is growing out of reach for normal Americans every year.

But while our current health care system actively creates inequality, Medicare for All offers an opportunity to reduce it.

There's a concept called "job lock." Think of someone who hates their job and works just hard enough at it because of their health care benefits. There's probably a job out there somewhere that they're better suited for and would be more passionate about working for, but they need health insurance for themselves or for their family. Not only are they locked in, but their boss has them rather than someone who actually would give it their all. There's a situation that would make both the boss and employee better off, but it's unattainable. This is inefficient for all involved.

Our current system also disadvantages small businesses, which are in a much less competitive position to recruit talent because of how expensive these benefits are. More employees could help them grow their business, but when it comes to attracting employees, really talented ones expect health care. Having to trade-off between hiring more workers to increase

---
84 Cecere, "45,000 Deaths Annually."
85 Palosky and Ducat, "Benchmark Employer Survey."

productivity and the increase in premium costs is an unenviable position. In contrast to double-digit cost increases every year, a predictable tax bill sounds pretty great from a business perspective. Their employees would also be more likely to give their all during business hours if they're healthy and not worried about looming debt. Additionally, having fewer people in the community with health care debt is more people who can spend money at their stores.

Where society really misses out on potential gains, however, is entrepreneurship lock. Just as someone might be locked into their job rather than switching to another for fear of losing their insurance, we have evidence that employer-provided insurance "discourages workers from turning to self-employment."[86] Starting a business is a big enough financial risk without the added fear of having to pay medical bills after getting hit by a bus.

Innovation in our society is playing with one hand behind its back. When only a small proportion of the country has the means to tinker around in the garage to come up with new business ideas, the country's potential is limited. If you're a country that wants to drive innovation, you want to have as many people as possible able to experiment with ideas that could change the world. Yes, starting a business is a risk, and wealthier people would still be able to weather that risk better under Medicare for All. But taking the loss of health care out of the mental equation that people will need to do when evaluating that risk levels the playing field a bit and increases the number of people who can take it. Creating

---

86 Baker, "Job Lock."

a larger pool of people to think up next-generation ideas effectively doubles or triples the odds that one will succeed. Think of it as creating a nationwide startup incubator.

Not only will this benefit the entrepreneur who can reap the benefits of their new business, but also the rest of society who takes advantage of their innovation. Those new companies will also create more, better-paying jobs, which will have a better shot of attracting talent at first because they don't have to compete on health care benefits.

Lowering this barrier could drive the next wave of American entrepreneurship, one fueled by and for people from all economic backgrounds.

It's time for Medicare for All.

CHAPTER 5

WELCOME TO THE JUNGLE

How did we let PETA types take over the environmentalist movement?

By the time of An Inconvenient Truth, the documentary on global warming, environmentalists or climate change activists had been relegated in our minds to eggheads, people with low iron levels, and vegetarians with a vengeance. But taking care of the environment was not a party-line issue through Nixon, who passed the National Environmental Policy Act, which established some of our first environmental standards. If I were to guess, most of the Republican elites understand climate change is real. Ted Cruz is a pretty intelligent human being, for example. He's just slimy enough to pretend he doesn't understand the severity of the issues because his career depends on it.

Negative associations with environmentalists are pretty wild when you consider the fact that the National Parks were created by Teddy Roosevelt, who cared about preserving nature because he wanted to continue being able to travel the world to kill giant creatures. Environmentalists gave up the image of a grizzled outdoorsman—someone traveling across the rugged terrain to pit himself against nature. You know, a badass.

America has a unique conception of itself based on how its landmass was acquired. Manifest Destiny caused a massive amount of Native suffering, but the idea of a westward expansion, picking up your life, and going into nature is deep-seated in America's cultural psyche. Why do you think we still care so much about the cowboy?

One of the things I learned from the Trump years is how tied together people's identity and political affiliations are. The Trump supporters I've spoken with have all listed "strength" as a positive and perceive all of his actions through this lens of self-assuredness as making Americans stronger. In contrast, liberals were viewed as meek and weak.

The reason that so many people don't believe in climate change is, of course, a decades-long disinformation campaign that was established by oil companies before it was picked up by conservative news sources. By this point, it's deeply ingrained in the conservative identity. Denying climate change isn't just what you think; it's part of who you are. You aren't one of the sheep who believes something is a fact just because 95 percent of scientists say so. You're an individualist who can see past their lies and listens to the 5 percent of scientists who go against the grain. The fact that those 5 percent of scientists have their studies paid for by vested interests like oil companies or other polluters doesn't register when a key part of your identity rests on that logic.

You can't just yell at someone until they drop a major part of their identity. I've tried. It doesn't work. You have to replace it.

Environmental issues used to be much simpler. You could see that someone was dumping waste into a river, preventing people from drinking the water. You could see that there was so much smoke it turned into acid rain, preventing people from breathing outdoors. So, simple problems got simple solutions with the Clean Water Act and the Clean Air Act.

Climate change is slightly more complex, in part because you can't look out your window and see it every day of the year. It's a long-term issue, and we have short attention spans. People can look at pollution on a beach and feel on an emotional level it's gross, but when it comes to understanding that Texas now has to deal with blizzards because of something called a jet stream, they can't compute.

My view on environmental policy isn't just "Tell people they're Teddy Roosevelt and call it a day." But you need to make that association for people so that they can replace the old part of their identities with something better. As it stands, few people are rushing to make the Democratic slogan of "Believe in science" part of their identities.

Call it the climate or call it the environment: Keeping Earth livable is a winning issue; you just need to talk about it in the right way.

IF WE FIX THE CLIMATE AND WE DIDN'T NEED TO, WE'RE ALL RICH.

The Green New Deal got a lot of flak because its opponents realized how powerful it was. For those out of the loop, the Green New Deal or GND is a proposal to tackle the worst emissions that humans create through a jobs program. The main points are to get the United States to become emissions-neutral before 2050 and create "millions of good, high-wage jobs" by upgrading the nation's infrastructure and meeting all of our energy needs through clean, renewable energy.[87] The idea of a Green New Deal has been around for a while, but the one most people talk about was originally a nonbinding resolution to establish America's intent to do this. The phrase has now taken on a life of its own and can mean someone's goal to implement any of these programs.

While it's more of an overarching set of goals than it is a law in and of itself, it's still the most ambitious set of goals out there that I know of. Let's work with the outline that we've got and then settle in on the details. It helps that people like each of the policies that made up the New Deal. It covered a lot of ground—everything from regulating the stock market and guaranteeing bank deposits to offering credit at fair rates to farmers. Besides helping us get out of the Great Depression, it's most famous for having a massive jobs program. Roosevelt paid Americans to build public infrastructure and preserve our national resources through groups like the Civilian Conservation Corps.[88] It was influenced by an economist named John Maynard Keynes, who had the idea

---

87 Ocasio-Cortez, "H.Res.109."
88 Stoller, *Goliath*, 106.

that when a government invests in its people, everybody gets great returns. Revolutionary stuff.

Roosevelt's New Deal paid American workers, many of whom couldn't find work because of the Great Depression, to build a huge amount of public goods, highways, hospitals, dams, schools, you name it.[89] Not only did Americans have good-paying jobs, but they were then able to use the money they earned to buy food, housing, and other things they needed but previously couldn't afford. Paying people helped those people put money back into the economy, and we got massive amounts of infrastructure out of it. Not bad!

Now picture that but focused on putting Americans to work building a new, renewable energy infrastructure. Within two years, the original New Deal employed twenty million people.[90] Now consider the fact that the American population in 1936 was a little over a third of the American population in 2021.[91] Putting tens of millions of Americans to work in good-paying jobs that benefit the public good would be popular at any time, much less during a downturn that put millions of people out of work. How is this not front and center?

On the off chance that climate change really is a hoax made up by the Chinese, and February's blizzard in Texas was a mass hallucination, people still like money. People also tend to like people who give them money. High-wage jobs aren't just good for the people with money in their pocket. It also

---

89 Blitz, "When America's Infrastructure Saved Democracy."
90 Deeben, "Family Experiences and New Deal Relief."
91 "US Population: From 1900," *Demographia*.

pushes the labor market to pay everyone else higher wages to compete for talent. Those people with increased wages then have money to spend on shit they couldn't afford previously, creating demand for goods.

Public investments in green technology also have the opportunity for massive payoffs for Americans.

The COVID pandemic reveals a lot about how people view themselves in the context of their society. When people thought masks were to protect themselves, everyone was on board. Once it came out that masks were really to keep everyone else safe, the tide turned, and Fox and company began a really effective anti-mask campaign. Mask use dropped, infection rates went up, and all of a sudden, doing your part to keep grandma safe was dropped.

Clearly, the era of the Greatest Generation going months without meat for the war effort is gone. People are so in their bubble that they have less of a sense of self-sacrifice. Now it's people's God-given right to skip the mask and cough in each other's faces.

Americans have always had an individualistic streak, but I think this is going to be a dominant force for the foreseeable future. Not that this is anything new. Public participation in groups from churches to bowling leagues has been declining for decades. It's little wonder that people who don't participate in groups have trouble seeing themselves as a member of a group. However, this is a subject for another book.

As much as it breaks my heart, I don't think you're going to win too many new votes by appealing to people's morality here.

The eggheads are already on board, and 626 environmental groups signed a letter in favor of it. Everyone else needs to see that it's in their financial interest to do so.

So, if we adopt the Green New Deal, even if we didn't need to, we'll all be much better off.

On the other hand, if we don't work to fix the climate and it turns out that we needed to, we're all fucked. The worst-case scenario is pretty easy to comprehend: The planet gets too hot, returns to the burning ball of hell fire it was billions of years ago, and everyone dies.

Dramatic, I know. But if things don't get quite that bad, life as we know it will still go through a blender. We can even see it starting now with the increase of extreme weather. Morgan Stanley (known servants of the liberal agenda) issued a report that showed extreme weather caused $650 billion worth of damage across the world from 2016–2019. North America took the brunt of that damage, suffering about two-thirds of that cost.[92]

The Economist (a magazine dedicated to the resurrection of the Soviet Union) projects that the worldwide global economy will be 3 percent smaller by 2050 due to our lack of climate resilience.[93] Given the track that we're on now, the amount of change we can expect, and the provisions we've put in place, the loss is at least several trillion dollars. In case my sarcasm

---

92 DiChristopher, "Climate Disasters Cost $650 Billion."
93 "Global Economy Will Be 3 Percent Smaller," *Economist Intelligence Unit*.

didn't translate, both Morgan Stanley and the Economist lean toward fiscal conservativism. If anything, these numbers are on the low end. Losing trillions of dollars is the best-case scenario if we don't do anything.

We've covered a best-case scenario (jobs exist, but climate change doesn't) and a worst-case scenario (humans don't exist). Let's wrap this section up with what a middle-case scenario looks like. America as we know it relies upon energy and cheap toys; we've either imposed sanctions to secure our entitlement or declared war over these resources. If we don't develop the green technology that could lead to energy independence, we will still be dependent on oil-rich countries like Saudi Arabia or eventual green power giant China. As for everyday life, most of the countries we rely on for cheap goods are at risk of becoming inhospitable due to climate change. Our top five sources of clothing, for example, are China, Vietnam, India, Bangladesh, and Mexico.[94] If our trading partners go underwater, the cheap prices we rely on will go out the window.

CLIMATE FREEDOM

"The analysis assumes, based on the preponderance of evidence available, that significant changes in climate have already occurred, likely to worsen in the years ahead. The study did not look to ascribe causation to climate change (man-made or natural), as causation is distinct from effects and not pertinent to the approximately fifty-year horizon

---

94 "United States Textiles and Clothing Imports," *World Integrated Trade Solution*.

considered for the study. The study does, however, assume that human behavior can mitigate both the size and consequences of negative impacts that result from climate change."[95]

Don't talk about whether or not it's our fault. Just talk about what we're going to do to stop making it worse. At least, that's the Army's take on it.

The above quote is from "Implications of Climate Change for the US Army," a report commissioned by the Chairman of the Joint Chiefs of Staff Mark Milley. The report outlines how climate change poses a threat to national security. Weather changes will leave tens or hundreds of millions of people without food and water due to crops being unsuited to the new climate and water drying up. Those people will still need to eat and will leave their countries looking for somewhere to live. The downside of mass migrations is that they've been a big source of conflict in recent history. Rising sea levels will eliminate many sources of fresh water, and hot weather makes clean water more important. That same heat will also put pressure on our power grids, which will mean less supply of power as people need more of it for things like air conditioning. Any potential power outage in that situation would cripple the economy. Finally, warm weather provides breeding grounds for more insects and tropical diseases, which will pose an obvious threat.[96]

Reading this paper is eerie: It's dispassionate and apolitical and talks about all of the ways a hotter earth will change

---

95 Brosig et al., "Implications of Climate Change."
96 Ibid.

life as we know it. From the outset, it essentially says, "We can't say why this is happening. All we can say that it is." It's like being a kid, and no one in your house will use the word "divorce," but you know that Dad's been sleeping at a hotel for weeks now, and it doesn't seem like he's coming back.

At the end of the day, climate security means freedom. Freedom from the apocalypse trumps all other freedoms. If your land no longer supports the crops you've grown for generations, or you don't have water to grow them with, you're going to go hungry. It's really hard to live your life when food is out of the question, and that's before you account for new bugs and tropical diseases. If half the world's landmass becomes unlivable, you aren't free to live your life. If a vicious cycle annihilates human life, we aren't free to . . . well, you get the point.

Here's an absolutely insane idea: Next time you find yourself in a lighthearted conversation about climate change, use Fox News. Don't use Tucker Carlson's confused-looking face but take the tone that he uses to describe immigrants, or Antifa, or pregnant women in the army, and replace those words with, say, greenhouse gasses. "Blood and soil" arguments are reprehensible when used to describe fellow human beings, but clearly, the tone strikes a chord with a large number of Americans. Let's try it out:

"Climate change is coming to take your job."

"Greenhouse gases are ruining this neighborhood. Can't even recognize it when you walk down the street."

"We must protect the homeland. That's why I drive an electric car."

The skeptic in me thinks that the idea of climate refugees would be a pretty effective message for the Fox News crowd. Picture a thirty-second ad running during Hannity that says, "Climate change is real. As the earth warms, the poorest countries will become inhabitable first. Those people are going to need somewhere to go. Weak on climate is weak on immigration." New emissions regulations would be passed overnight.

Whoever alerts the "They will not replace us crowd" to the millions of climate refugees that the army predicts would help solve the problem overnight. There's a pent-up aggression and lack of nuance that can be spoken to. They need a war.

War is primal. Whatever we're at war with is bad. War on Drugs? Drugs are clearly bad. War on Crime? Hell yeah, brother. So how do you go to war with the atmosphere heating up? Just pick a simple word and then pick a fight with it. Any policies after that will be a much easier sell. How does the War on Pollution sound? After all, it's not like the War on Drugs was Richard Nixon curb-stomping a crack pipe. Hell, if you really wanted to, you could throw in the fact that China has been leading the world in green energy investment for years now and go for Fox News Bingo.

But we have a lesson to be learned here to convince people who aren't white supremacists, too. Climate change is a matter of national security. Tens of millions of climate refugees will be leaving behind failed states in inhospitable regions that would require billions in American federal aid. Failed states would lead to power vacuums. Power vacuums are breeding grounds for extremists, who will likely have beef with large, rich nations who knew about this danger and continued to refuse to curb their emissions.

I understand why some people can't wrap their heads around it enough to care. It's scary, it's science-y, and it's abstract. The same thing happens to me when people talk about musical theory. So, stop talking about it in a way that makes people's eyes glaze over, or they're going to tune out.

CHAPTER 6

CONSCIOUS OF CLASS

What kind of economic system do we have in America? Every single person will tell you, whether with pride or disdain, that we are a capitalist society. Some of those people will even tell you that capitalism makes us freer than other countries.

Funny enough, in the same way that people can't really define socialism besides whatever is convenient for them at that moment, people struggle to define capitalism.

Let's look at the word itself: "capital" "ism." Okay, so a system built around capital. But what is capital? Capital is what we use to make shit. Usually, it's the land, machines, and equipment we use in factories, but can also include the massive amounts of assets we need to make those factories. It's a little more nebulous of a concept now, but that's what it was historically.

From a historical perspective, capitalism is certainly preferable to the economic system that came before it, known as **feudalism**. Under feudalism, essentially all wealth and power are determined by birth, as there's very little social mobility. If you were born a nobleman, you would stay a nobleman and keep your land and wealth. Noblemen were allowed to own that land because it was ceded to them by royalty in exchange for their loyalty. (Bonus points if you tell people you're king because God made it so.) If you were born as a peasant or serf, you were tied to the land you were born on because that's how you survive. They didn't have a labor market per se; you farmed on the nobleman's land, gave a portion of that to the nobleman so he could stay wealthy, and then ate the rest. Land ownership is wealth and power, so their economic system and political system were essentially the same things.[97]

Eventually, people get good enough at shipbuilding that they can sail to faraway places. Your wool and weapons aren't especially valuable in your hometown, where everyone has them, but if you can go far away to trade, they are more valuable. The spices and silk (and eventually slaves) you get from other lands will be even more valuable in your home, so you can afford more goods to trade. Suddenly, a new class of wealthy people emerges who weren't born rich. To compete and stay rich, the craftier nobles began clearing the serfs who grow food off their land so that they can focus on goods that are valuable overseas, like wool. Those serfs now transition from working the land they were born on to selling their labor—creating a labor market.[98]

Boom, a basic history of how feudalism turned to capitalism in Europe (obviously this is oversimplifying a lot of things, but if you're curious, you can find better explanations that go more in depth).

---

97 Varoufakis, *Talking to My Daughter about the Economy*, 40.
98 Ibid., 42.

CAPITALISM, HOORAY!

Good news: Economic classes aren't entirely designated by birth anymore. Well, if you're born wealthy within the last few hundred years under a capitalist system, you are pretty likely to stay wealthy. Even today, being born wealthy is the biggest indicator of your future success in life, even greater than intelligence.[99] But, it's no longer hard-coded into society that someone born poor isn't allowed to become rich.

Bad news: We still have a class system. By definition, there is a 99 percent chance someone isn't going to be born into the 1 percent of wealthiest people. Capitalism is still by default an unequal system. If we define our system by who owns the factories, land, and wealth, only a minority can be in the upper class; someone still needs to work in the factories, after all. When the race is defined by who owns capital, and you don't own capital, you're losing that race. It's like the old joke that says, "If you don't own the factory, you aren't a capitalist. You're a laborer with Stockholm Syndrome."

To clarify, this isn't a book on socialism. My goal is to take stock of how our society is organized and how we can improve on it. You can't just call anything that even thinks about a better way to live socialism. Being unable to reflect on and criticize our economic system is censorship bordering on totalitarianism. It's so "1984" of you.

Some philosophers have claimed that all of human history is just the wealthy classes and the poor classes struggling against each other. The wealthy want to be wealthy, and the

---

99 Carnevale et al., "Born to Win, Schooled to Lose."

poor want to, well, not starve. Economics is the study of how people obtain scarce resources and has a big impact on our political system. Being unable to criticize how people obtain or keep those resources might show you the people who are running the system.

Next chapter, we're going to talk about the state of inequality in America. The purpose of this chapter was to prime you with the idea that class distinctions in America don't exist in a vacuum. We are all part of historical trends, and no one knows what's coming next. All I ask is that you keep these trends in mind as you continue to read.

CHAPTER 7

GILDED AGE MERRY-GO-ROUND: THE BIG, SEXY ECON CHAPTER

Is it the natural state of our society to result in the billionaires and the broke?

If you think, "Yes, and that's a problem," feel free to skip this part.

If you think, "Yes, and that's a good thing," seek help.

Everyone else—let's talk about the distribution of wealth in our country.

Get by with a little help from my Trends.

How much of our nation's income do you think the wealthy take home?

For a frame of reference, think of your net worth. From one year to the next, it will change based on your income from work, which will include health benefits, how your stock portfolio and everything else you own increases in value, and dividends you get from stocks. It will also change based on things you own, decreasing in value. If you own a car, it's going to be less valuable next year because it's older and has more miles on it. You're also going to buy things like groceries, which will slightly decrease your income. Now do this for the whole nation, businesses included.[100]

Then write down what percentage you think our nation's wealth increase goes to the richest people.

As of 2018, the top 1 percent take home 20 percent of the nation's income. That is to say, for every dollar that the United States gets richer by, 1 percent of people get 20 cents.

Okay, time for the same experiment: How much of our nation's income do you think the bottom 50 percent of our people take home?

As of 2018, the poorest 50 percent of Americans take home 12 percent of the nation's income. For every dollar, the United States gets richer by, half of the people split 12 cents.

Surely it was always this extreme, though, right? Like, the rich are rich because they earn more money, and that's how it's always been, right? No? Fuck.

---

100 Saez and Zucman, *Triumph of Injustice*, 2.

Since at least 1978, the rich have been taking home more of the nation's income almost every year. In fact, the 1 percent share of the nation's income has doubled in that time. In 1978, the 1 percent took home 10 percent while the bottom half took home 20 percent.[101]

You might also note that that the amount the bottom half lost is about the amount that the richest 1 percent gained. This makes intuitive sense because the percentage of income taken home adds up to 100 percent, so it's a zero-sum game. One group getting more means another group gets less. What doesn't make intuitive sense is how this is allowed to happen.

While inequality is a growing problem, it's not growing anywhere else as quickly as in America: "In Western Europe the top 1 percent income share has increased by two percentage points (instead of ten points as in America), to reach 12 percent today. The bottom 50 percent income share has declined two percentage points, from 24 percent to 22 percent." The poorest half of Western Europeans are still taking home more of their national income than their American counterparts were in 1978.[102]

A similar trend exists for how much of the nation's wealth each group owns. (If income is the change in wealth each year, think of wealth as the total value at the end of the year).

Just after World War II, the richest 1 percent and the bottom 90 percent owned the same proportion of the nation's wealth,

---

101 Ibid, 7.
102 Ibid.

a little under 30 percent each. For the next few decades, the bottom 90 percent earned more of that wealth every year, and the 1 percent had less of it every year. This is due to a few reasons that we'll explore in a bit, but for now, you can chalk it up to high incomes for laborers because of collective bargaining, a strong safety net, and progressive taxation. The 1 percent wealth ownership bottomed out at 25 percent around 1980 and has steadily climbed since. The bottom 90 percent wealth ownership topped out at 40 percent in the mid-'80s and has fallen almost ever since.[103]

Part of this is due to income trends. Post-World War II, average income growth was pretty spread out. Almost every income percentile grew 2 percent on average. Since 1980, growth has been centered at the very top: "For the highest 0.1 percent of earners, incomes have grown 320 percent since 1980; for the top 0.01 percent, incomes have grown by as much as 430 percent. And for the tip-top 0.001 percent—the richest 2,300 Americans—incomes have grown by more than 600 percent." In contrast, "The average pretax income of the bottom 50 percent, which amounts to $18,500 in 2018, has barely increased: adjusted for inflation, it was around $17,500 in the late 1970s. This corresponds to an annual growth rate of 0.1 percent over four decades."[104]

The end result of this is that the richest 1 percent of Americans owned about 40 percent of the wealth in America before the pandemic.

---

103 Ibid, 98.

104 Ibid, 164.

Since the pandemic, billionaires alone have gotten $1.3 trillion richer, or an increase of 44 percent, since March 2020. To clarify, that is billionaires alone, not millionaires. To be a member of the 1 percent, your income would have to be around $400,000. This $1.3 trillion went to just the top 0.0001 percent or 664 people.[105] Working people lost that much money in May.[106] The $1.3 trillion that billionaires gained could be used to give every man, woman, and child in America $3,900.

While this is a shocking amount of money, it's also part of a larger trend. So how did we get here?

TRICKLE DOWN DOESN'T WORK—OR HOW DID WE GET HERE?

"What we've found is if you cut taxes for the rich, it doesn't lead to economic growth or lower unemployment. The only thing that happens really is that inequality goes up."

This is Dr. Julian Limberg, economist and Lecturer in Public Policy at King's College London. Dr. Limberg coauthored one of the most important economic studies of the last few years titled "Economic Consequences of Major Tax Cuts for the Rich," published by the International Inequalities Institute at the London School of Economics and Political Science.[107] We had the opportunity to connect over Zoom this February.

---

105 Collins, "Updates."

106 Cohen, "US Workers Have Lost $1.3 Trillion."

107 Hope and Limberg, "Economic Consequences of Tax Cuts for the Rich."

Limberg and his coauthor, Dr. David Hope, took data from eighteen countries in the Organization for Economic Co-Operation and Development, measured periods where the tax code became less progressive and measured the effects with a difference-in-differences model examining "the top 1 percent share of pretax national income."[108]

In short, they looked at countries like the US, UK, and South Korea, examined when they cut taxes on the rich and saw if rich people in one country got richer than rich people in another country.

"It's a bit more complex than that, but the basic idea is that we compared countries which are similar with the one difference being that some had these tax cuts and others didn't have them, and then see how the outcomes varied, like more growth or lower unemployment, or different trajectories of inequality," he said during our Zoom interview.

The research referenced Ronald Reagan's two major tax cuts during his time in office, in 1981 and 1986. Together, they dropped the top tax rate from 70 percent to 28 percent.[109]

Tax cuts are usually sold as a way to grow the economy. Giving the rich free rein would allow them to invest in jobs, lower unemployment, and create more wealth for everybody. The idea of all that money trickling down to normal people sounds great in theory. The problem is that this doesn't work in reality. Hope and Limberg studied thirty major tax

---

108 Ibid.
109 Ingraham, "Top Tax Rate Has Been Cut Six Times."

cuts in these eighteen countries over the course of decades. What happened?

The effects of tax cuts on GDP growth couldn't be found.

The effects of tax cuts on unemployment couldn't be found.

The only effects of the tax cuts that they could prove were that the richest people in each country took home much more of their nation's income. Letting the rich shirk, their taxes lead to more inequality.[110]

This makes sense if you think about it because cutting taxes on the rich is supposed to create inequality. The big issue is that this inequality is supposed to help everybody, and it simply doesn't.

Reagan lied to us. Now we're footing the bill.

WHAT ABOUT AN EXAMPLE?
This can be hard to imagine, so let's see what it looks like in practice.

Based on publicly available records, we know Warren Buffet gets paid $100,000 in his role as CEO of Berkshire Hathaway.[111] However, his net worth is currently $100 billion.[112] Did he somehow work 1 million years? No—separate from

---

110 Ibid.
111 Berger, "Warren Buffett."
112 Li, "Warren Buffett's Net Worth."

the work he did for his job, he owned something, and it increased in value. Maybe you already knew this, not really groundbreaking stuff that Warren Buffet owns stocks. When stocks or land, or even Bitcoin, increase in value, you pay a capital gains tax.

If you earned $75,000 a year and never spent a penny, it would take you 1,333,333 years and change to accumulate $100 billion dollars. More than a million years—it's such a crazy number it almost sounds ridiculous, like earning a gazillion pennies.

Of course, that's only if you held onto every dollar. Instead, the average consumer spent $61,224 in 2018 while making $78,635, according to the Bureau of Labor Statistics. This is total spending, so after housing, food, and y'know, living, the average person netted about $17,000.[113] Warren Buffett-level money might take a lot longer at that rate. (Working as an executive cuts this time down significantly. CEO compensation has grown by about 1,000 percent since 1978, while employee pay has grown by 11 percent over the same period. The average CEO now makes 271 times the salary of the average worker, up from twenty times the salary of the average worker in 1978).[114]

The key here is the capital gains tax. While Buffett gets taxed on his salary from Berkshire Hathaway, he doesn't get taxed on how much richer he is due to stocks until he sells them or dies. Despite the fact that he got almost $30 billion richer between September and March, he only gets taxed on his

---

113 "Consumer Expenditures in 2018," US Bureau of Labor Statistics.
114 Mishel and Schieder, "CEO Pay Remains High Relative."

$100,000 income.[115] If you want to pay less in taxes, you simply have to get really rich and then stop receiving much of a salary.

Is this the part where I tell you Warren Buffett isn't doing his part? Well . . . kinda.

For the first time in at least a century, capital income in America is taxed at a lower effective rate than labor income.[116] All income is either capital income or labor income. You can only make money by doing work or by owning something. Those are the only options. The average tax rate for all labor income in America is just under 30 percent. The average tax rate for all capital income is 26 percent.[117] Americans get taxed more for working than they do for owning shit.

Why are labor income and capital income taxed at different rates? Rich people don't want it to change.

On an intuitive level, it seems like a scam. Taxes should work as starting the year with a certain amount of wealth, and over the course of the year, if you have more wealth coming in, you are taxed on that amount. Instead, the wealthy get taxed at about half the rate people get taxed for their actual jobs.

Now consider that just under half of Americans (45 percent) aren't in the stock market; only 14 percent are invested in

---

115 Li, "Warren Buffett's Net Worth."
116 Saez and Zucman, *Triumph of Injustice*, 93.
117 Ibid.

individual stocks. The richest 10 percent of Americans own 84 percent of the stock wealth in the country.[118]

This is what's known as a regressive tax system. Rich people pay less of their wealth in taxes than poor people do. In contrast, a progressive tax system is one in which rich people pay more of their taxes than poor people do. Regressive tax systems end up with rich people getting richer, while progressive tax systems balance the playing field. We are seeing the effects of a regressive tax system now.

Interestingly (in a morbid way), state and local taxes are partially to blame for this fact: "On average, the poorest 20 percent of taxpayers spend 11.4 percent of their income on state and local taxes, which is 50 percent higher than the 7.4 percent average effective tax rate for the top 1 percent," according to the Institute on Taxation and Economic Policy.[119] Four percent might not seem like a huge difference until you realize that's almost half of what the rich pay in that category period. In practice, this can look like a state like Florida, which has the third most regressive tax code. Because there's no income tax, poor people and rich people pay the same amount of income tax, 0 percent. The poorest 20 percent of people pay about three times as much of their income in property taxes as the richest 1 percent do. If you make less than $19,000 in Florida, you will pay about 3.9 percent of your income in property taxes, while your counterpart, who makes over half a million dollars a year, will pay 1.3 percent of their income. Where this gets really extreme is sales and

---

118 Ghilarducci, "Most Americans."

119 "Fairness Matters," Institute on Taxation and Economic Policy.

excise taxes. The poorest 20 percent of people will pay 8.7 percent of their income in sales taxes, which is almost ten times higher than the 0.9 percent of income that the richest 1 percent pay.[120] (Take groceries, for example. Even if you make over half a million dollars a year, there's no way you could eat twenty-five times as much food as someone making $20,000. Because you buy similar amounts of food, it takes up a lot less of your income.) When it comes to regressive tax policies, Florida is the rule more so than it is the exception.

THE UPSHOT

Now we know that letting the rich avoid doing their part doesn't work. Hopefully, there's one easy answer of what we should tax them at to level the playing field, right? Unfortunately, Dr. Limberg thinks the answer is up to us. "There's this whole economics debate about optimal tax rates and so on. I think de facto; it's a political question. Where's the political support for that?" he asked.

"You would expect inequality to be self-correcting. If inequality goes up, then measures to reduce inequality would also go up. But there's a broken link [between these two]." So, what causes this broken link?

1. Power—the obvious answer. If the wealthy are overrepresented in politics and are more likely to have their voices heard, their wishes are more likely to be put into place. There's a lot of academic work being done to show that the wealthy have outsized influence, but you don't need me

---

120 "Florida," Institute on Taxation and Economic Policy.

to explain how politicians hoping to stay in office can be swayed by expensive fundraisers in their honor.

2. Unperceived Inequality—people might not realize just how unequal the system is. But humans are notoriously bad at dealing with giant numbers. For an experiment, think about how your life would change if you had $100 million. Now imagine having ten times that amount of money. You would then only have $10 billion. You would need nineteen of those $10 billion piles to have as much money as Jeff Bezos.

3. Perceptions of the Economy—**let's expand on this.**

PERCEPTIONS OF THE ECONOMY

"If people think less redistribution and less tax progressively is actually good for the economy, they might not want more redistributive changes. This might be changing, but it is changing very slowly (we're also interested in why this is changing so slowly)," as Dr. Lindberg told me.

Political Scientists Kenneth Scheve and David Stasavage wrote Taxing the Rich: A History of Fiscal Fairness in the United States and Europe, a book that examined the reason why people think taxing the rich is fair or unfair throughout history. Usually, this debate is around whether or not their wealth and taxes were deserved or not. What really triggers progressive taxation is when people perceive that rich people are getting unfair advantages.

One example of this was the World Wars. Demand for certain goods and raw materials skyrocketed, so rich people made huge amounts of money while being less likely to go to war themselves. Everyone else got pissed, and taxes rose to reflect this fact. When WWI started, the top marginal income tax rate in America was 7 percent. By the end, it was 77 percent. The same thing happened in Canada, with the top rate rising from 21.9 percent to 72.5 percent.[121]

This is what they call "compensatory demands." If there's the perception that this is unfair and the rich are treated beneficially that might actually trigger more redistribution.

For a modern-day example, imagine that the government ordered people to stay at home, and their only option was to order things online, so some kind of store that sold everything online would make a lot of money. Whoever owned this so-called "everything store" would become massively wealthy because it's people's only real option. If people realized that this everything store got rich because of something out of their control and then paid zero dollars in federal taxes, they might want to increase taxes on that company and its owner. It sounds impossible, but it would be Amazon.

Scheve and Stasavage said that one of the most frequent causes for this is war, but not all types: "Our argument does not apply to all wars; it applies to conflicts of mass mobilization in which a substantial proportion of the population are required to fight the war. In cases where a war is instead fought with a small portion of the population, potentially with individuals drawn primarily from groups lower down the socioeconomic

---

121 Scheve and Stasavage, "Conscription of Wealth," 11.

ladder, there will be fewer people likely to demand policies that equalize the burden of a war."[122]

This sounds dark for our cause. The only time people realize they're getting screwed are when you send enough of them off to die while some sit home and get rich. Additionally, warfare has been moving away from total war toward limited warfare due to drones and other technology. As long as the rich and powerful don't lead us into war and throw people enough scraps, they'll be placated.

On the other hand, a pandemic like the current one could be the right opportunity. Some people are profiting massively off of it, with an unimaginable rise in riches for the wealthy. Then there's what you can think of as the twenty-first-century version of the middle class—the people who can afford to work from home and have their groceries delivered or afford to Uber Eats their dinner every night. They're annoyed that they have to stay home, but their lifestyle isn't threatened.

Finally, you have the people actually affected by this pandemic, say, restaurant workers who are out of jobs and pushed into the gig economy. Some of whom will shift to an Uber Eats delivery job or even an OnlyFans (this isn't to shame OnlyFans creators, but the fact that the number of creators on the platform almost tripled from March to December has to make you stop and think).[123]

---

122 Ibid, 7.
123 "OnlyFans Statistics," Influencer Marketing Hub.

When I look at Scheve and Stasavage's work, I see that the only thing stopping people from demanding fairer taxes is that they have to realize they're getting screwed and hear that other people realize it, too.

During one lecture, Scheve pointed to the fact that in a society like our own, people think they should be taxed as equals, but the question of what "as equals" means changes over time. Should we pay based on our ability to pay? Should we all pay the same rate? Or if some people are getting preferential treatment, should we make up for it by taxing them more?[124]

The point of this chapter isn't to answer those questions, but rather to point out that when people tell you that there's an economic reason to avoid taxing the rich or to not raise the minimum wage, or do anything but give the rich everything they ask for, they're full of shit. These are issues that we decide as a society: What are the rules for playing along in our society? Trickle-down is bullshit, and you're allowed to have an opinion.

The first step is to have people realize this. The second step is to fight for it.

If one person says it, they might think you're crazy. If fifty people a day start saying it, well, they might just think it's a movement. All you have to do is join in.

---

124 Scheve and Stasavage, "Taxing the Rich."

CHAPTER 8

SPLIT DOWN THE MIDDLE: DEMAND-SIDE JESUS

"When Henry Ford's grandson gave labor union leader Walter Reuther a tour of the company's new, automated factory, he jokingly asked, 'Walter, how are you going to get those robots to pay your union dues?' Without missing a beat, Reuther answered, 'Henry, how are you going to get them to buy your cars?'"[125]

Most people know that the economy isn't working for them and don't need to know the economics behind that fact to understand it. You're welcome to skip this part. If you're curious as to why more money in the hands of more Americans is a good thing, let's press on.

---

125 Bregman, *Utopia for Realists*, 200.

DEMAND DRIVES THE ECONOMY

Anyone who has even looked at the cover of an economics textbook can tell you that the basics of economics are supply and demand. In an over-simplified world, the price of things is determined by how many of them are being sold and how many people want to buy them.

For almost as long as economics has been a field, people have understood that the main driving force in the economy is demand.

At some point in the '70s, a really good propagandist figured out a new way to spread the idea that businesses were the unsung martyrs of our world and needed to be unleashed from the tyranny of taxes that held us back as a society.

Unfortunately, this is a lot like a fox describing how hen houses don't actually keep the chickens safe.

Think of your own place in the economy. When you have money, you use it to buy things. Maybe it's housing, maybe it's a nice dinner, maybe it's a PS5. Other people like you are able to afford that PS5, too, because times are good. The amount of people buying PS5s allows Mom & Pop's Electronic Shop to put more products on the shelves, like new games or even a surround sound system. They, in turn, demand more goods from their suppliers, who can also develop and sell more goods while also hiring more employees. As long as everyone has money, the economy can keep growing.

On the other hand, think about what happens when you don't have money. You won't buy as much stuff, so Mom

& Pop can't sell as much, so they don't keep the shelves as stocked, so Sony can't develop new games and might have to lay off some employees, who in turn can't afford to spend money. The economy starts to shrink because people can't afford to buy anything. Demand goes down, and the economy tanks.

Now think about what this looks like in a world where not as many people are working. This isn't far off—the most common job in America is a truck driver. Google, Tesla, and Uber are all working on ways to automate this job away, as well as countless other jobs. Forward progress is good in the long run, but there will be growing pains. What happens when you get rid of the most common job in thirty-five states? What are the trickle-up effects when the people who are put out of work can't afford to buy things?

Hell, let's take a recent example. What happens when fourteen million people go unemployed at the same time, like during COVID?[126] Eighty thousand businesses went under between March and July. Three-fourths of these are what we would call small businesses. Pretty frightening when you consider the fact half of all Americans work at companies with fewer than 500 employees.[127] While small companies go under, large corporations are able to lobby for tax cuts and bailouts. Boeing got an $862 million bailout in the first quarter.[128]

---

126 Kochhar, "Unemployment Rose Higher in Three Months."
127 Ngo, "Small Businesses Are Quietly Dying."
128 Herman, "Corporate America Reaps Windfalls."

The year-end COVID relief bill also gave businesses a $220 billion write-off.[129]

Have you ever noticed how we judge people for receiving government aid, never corporations? Obviously, people aren't bringing up those arguments against people on welfare in good faith, but think for a second how it would sound if we did the same thing for corporations:

"Corporations need an incentive to work. If they know that they're just going to get bailed out, when will they learn fiscal responsibility? You know, if you give them money, they're just going to blow it on luxuries like corporate jets for the CEO rather than necessities like paying their employees. They say they need these bailouts, but why did I see the Delta CEO get into a Porsche in the parking lot?"

We only do this to people who don't already have a lot of money. Even Democrats do it: Biden's $1.9 trillion COVID relief plan is set to give aid to seventeen million fewer Americans than Trump's bill, just to shave off 0.8 percent of the cost.[130] To put that ridiculous attempt at cost savings in perspective, $1.9 trillion minus $15 billion still rounds up to $1.9 trillion!

But even if you don't care about helping people, or the fact that you're giving away less money than your predecessor

---

129 "Congress Gives Rich and Powerful Bonuses," Americans for Tax Fairness.
130 Cochrane, "Democrats Narrow Stimulus Payments."

who botched the aid process, there's an argument to be made that giving away less money is bad economics.

WHO CARES?

The United States needs a return to Demand Side Economics. Rather than making sure we can make more goods, the focus should be on making sure we have people to buy those goods.

The rich have gotten away with a lot of huffing and puffing about how America needs them more than they need America. We've already seen that cutting taxes on the rich doesn't do anything for the economy but give rich people more money, and you already know intuitively that if rich people aren't paying their taxes, then you have to.

Most of the people telling you we need to cut the taxes on the rich are rich people.

The smartest way to make sure the economy keeps running is to put more money in the hands of the people who will actually spend it. Call it Trickle Up Economics. Think of your coronavirus stimulus money. What did you do with that $1,200? Lots of people paid off bills. Some people joined mail-order wine clubs. Some people joined lots of mail-order wine clubs. But the key thing to keep in mind here is that that stimulus money immediately went back into the economy.

The fancy term for this is the **velocity of money.** Basically, it's how quickly money gets spent when you give it to certain people. If money is the blood of the economy, you want it moving around, right? Usually, your blood only stops pumping during heart attacks or death. The same is true when money isn't moving through the economy, whether because people are hoarding it or because people don't have enough to spend.

This is the reason we should be reducing taxes for normal people while increasing them for the rich. **Diminishing marginal utility** is when people get less value out of something, the more of it that they get. Your first slice of pizza is going to make you really happy. Your tenth slice of pizza will not. This also applies to money. If I gave Mark Zuckerberg a million dollars, he would shrug and forget about it. Maybe buy some more Facebook stock with it if he has some spare time on a Sunday afternoon. On the other hand, if I gave you a million dollars, it would probably change your life. Policies that help normal people will have a much bigger effect than helping billionaires because normal people will go out and spend it.

More money given to the wealthy is just going to get stockpiled. You're limited in how many nice dinners you can treat yourself to. Even if he flew to a new three-star Michelin restaurant every night, Zuck literally couldn't consume enough food to use his money in a lifetime.

Now consider for a moment the 2017 tax cuts. Where did the bulk of that money disappear to?

"More than 60 percent of the tax savings went to people in the top 20 percent of the income ladder, according to the nonpartisan Tax Policy Center."[131]

---

131 Horsley, "After Two Years, Trump Tax Cuts Have Failed."

The real meat of the tax cut went to corporations, who saw their top rate fall from 35 percent to 21 percent, therefore reducing the corporate tax rate by about 40 percent. Supply-Side Jesus would tell us that these noble beasts, newly unshackled, would rise up and outperform, bringing in so much new business that they would surely pay even more in taxes for us all!

Unfortunately, that's not what happened. Corporate income tax collection fell by $135 billion, or almost 40 percent exactly.[132]

Those companies then used their new cash for a wave of stock buybacks that totaled $806 billion.[133] While a whopping 6 percent of companies used their cash for employee bonuses, it was outweighed by a massive wave of layoffs from companies like AT&T, General Motors, and McDonald's, each laying off thousands of employees.[134, 135] Middle-class people getting a tax cut of $850 doesn't mean much if they lose their jobs.

SOME CONTEXT

Let's now tie all of these pieces together. Trump's tax cuts are part of a forty-year trend toward cutting taxes on the rich and corporations. Over this period, working people have seen their income stagnate while the growth of the stock market goes to the wealthy. Working people who don't earn

---

132 Gale, "Did the 2017 Tax Cut Pay for Itself?"
133 Troise, "US Companies' Tax Windfall Fuels Record Share Buybacks."
134 "The JUST Capital Rankings on Corporate Tax Reform," *JUST Capital.*
135 Schaal, "These Companies Laid Off Large Numbers."

more money can't afford to buy things, and this is bad for everyone in the long run.

The really terrifying part comes from a study done by the National Bureau of Economic Research (NBER), a nonpartisan group that's been around since 1920 and is currently run by an MIT professor. In 2019, NBER published a paper titled "How the Wealth Was Won: Factors Shares as Market Fundamentals." The paper says that equity prices increased twice as much between 1989–2017 as between 1952–1988, but that 54 percent of this was due to "reallocation of rents to shareholders in a decelerating economy," with economic growth accounting for 24 percent of it. In contrast, 92 percent of equity growth was driven by economic growth.[136] I know, my eyes are glazing over too, but this is pretty shocking.

Basically, we have two periods of time: the post-war period and the Reagan years. In the post-war years, stocks and equity get more valuable by X percent, but almost all of it comes from real economic activity: People are building factories, processes are more efficient, and consumers are buying more stuff, so companies make more money. On the other hand, in the Reagan years, stocks and equity get more valuable by 2X percent, but only about a quarter of this is driven by real economic activity, like people buying more stuff. Where does the rest of this growth come from? Fifty-four percent comes from "factors share shock that reallocates the rewards of production without affecting the size of those rewards. Our estimates imply that the realizations of this shock persistently reallocated rents to shareholders and away from labor

---

136 Greenwald, Lettau, and Ludvigson, "How the Wealth Was Won."

compensation." The other 11 percent of this growth comes from "declining interest rates and a decline in risk premia."

Let's zoom in on that 54 percent. "Reallocating the rewards of production without affecting the size of those rewards" means that companies are making the same amount of money, but they're just changing who it's going to. Where are they reallocating it to? "To shareholders and away from labor compensation."[137] Companies are making roughly the same amount of money, but they're not giving it to the working people who work at those companies in the form of increased wages. Instead, that money is used to increase stock prices, partially through buybacks, which were illegal until 1982.

The first thing that you learn as an MBA is that Profit = Revenue - Costs. To maximize profits, you must minimize costs.

The second thing you learn as an MBA is that the easiest costs to try and reduce are taxes and wages to employees.

The macro trend that we see here is that working people don't see the benefits of their work because they are being distributed to stockholders, who are already likely to be wealthy. Wealthy people getting wealthier depends in large part on working people getting paid less. This isn't to shit talk the entire stock market. Sometimes you do have a new company that generates wealth by creating new ideas and innovation. But as a macroeconomic trend, relying on stagnant wages to boost equity prices isn't sustainable.

---

137 Ibid.

You probably already knew this. All it takes to figure this out is to look around and see the fact that minimum wage has been stuck at $7.25 since 2009 or that most people haven't gotten real raises in years to get that people don't see the benefits of growth. Workers are about 70 percent more productive since 1979 because of advances in technology like email. Wages, however, have only grown 12 percent in that same time.[138] That's a huge Productivity-Pay Gap, and that ~58 percent gap in productivity increase and wage increase is going to wealthy Americans.

Sure, any one rich person might benefit from taking siphoning off people's wages. But when the entire system is based around this, everyone suffers.

WHERE ARE WE GOING?

IN THE LONG-RUN, WE'RE ALL DEAD

The long-term implications of inequality are pretty spooky. An economist named Thomas Piketty is known for writing a book called Capital in the Twenty-First Century that only about fifteen people have read cover to cover. It's a massive book, but what you have to know is this:

<u>People are making more money off of their money than they have at any point in recent history.</u>

Why is this important? Imagine you're running a race on a long, flat road, but your opponent is allowed to start halfway

---

138 "The Productivity–Pay Gap," *Economic Policy Institute*.

to the finish line. If it's a long race and you're pretty fast, you could have a chance to catch up. It's not a big chance, but it's a chance! Now imagine the same race, where your opponent starts halfway to the finish line, but your opponent is riding a bike. While the distance disadvantage hurts you, you are never going to catch up because your opponent is going faster than you can run.

Some people are going to be born with more money, and that's a fact of life. But when you can't catch up no matter how hard you work, you will end up in a society where the rich stay rich forever. We're sold the idea that with hard work, anyone can overcome their background and make it big. If hard work doesn't give you a chance at a better life, we lose sight of the American dream.

This is the current track we're on. As everything stands, we will soon end up with a true American oligarchy.

Now think about how technology plays into this. Artificial Intelligence will make whoever owns the companies creating it fabulously wealthy, while automation will continue to put average people out of jobs. With truck drivers and retail workers already at risk of having their jobs eliminated due to automation, the economy will have fewer and fewer jobs that robots can't do while the rest of us compete for fewer and fewer positions. With fewer jobs available, people will race each other to the bottom by saying they'll work for less and less money. Normal people won't even be allowed to run the race. As political scientist Ian Bremmer said, "Technology has always created more jobs as long as you had things human beings could do [. . .] and that doesn't mean that we can no longer lead meaningful lives, but you have to change your model because capitalism is no longer about labor. The problem is that this is coming soon, soon, soon."[139] Capitalism has always had power struggles between capital and labor, but when there's no longer a need for labor, humans need to figure out what to do.

If we stay on this path, the people who are rich now will be so permanently, while the rest of us are stuck at the bottom with no class mobility. Eventually, AI will be intelligent enough to invent an even more powerful form of intelligence, one that humans can't create something to compete with. The American Dream goes past the Big Sleep and enters the Big Nightmare.

On the other hand, we have an opportunity for Artificial Intelligence to bring about an era of unimaginable human prosperity. When technology is more productive than humans at any imaginable task, we'll have no reason to work at a dead-end job or really anything that doesn't grow the human spirit. All humans are entitled to happy, fulfilled lives, and automation providing that future would be an incredible thing. As long as this isn't concentrated in the hands of a few people, I find no reason everyone can't be satisfied.

Almost a century ago, economist John Maynard Keynes was optimistically looking forward to the day when humans would work fifteen-hour weeks. To get to the spot where everyone's needs are fulfilled, however, we'll need "redistribution of money (basic income), of time (a shorter working

---

139 Justin Pemberton, "Capital in the Twenty-First Century."

week), of taxation (on capital instead of labor), and, of course, of robots."[140] It's not that having robots do all of our work is a bad thing. Work is unfulfilling for most people, and automating away tedious jobs would be a huge boon to society.

Standing in between us and this distant, rosy future are some tough conversations about how our society is organized. Piketty says there's one main option to get us to that point. It sounds crazy, but he says we'll need to start considering it to have any hope of a future.

BILLIONAIRE TAX

Before we get going, I want to define a term: ultrawealthy. I do not mean your uncle, who is a lawyer. I do not mean your cousin, who's a doctor. It's a nebulous term, but for most money managers, an Ultra High Net Worth Individual is one with a net worth of at least $30 million. For the sake of argument, you and I are going to define the ultrawealthy with over $50 million.

Taxes make people's eyes glaze over, and policy changes really quickly, so I'm not going to get in the weeds here. Senator Elizabeth Warren's billionaire tax is the most famous tax plan, so let's use that. It only affects people with $50 million or more, which is about 75,000 households.[141]

It only affects the amount of money they have over $50 million (that is, if you have $60 million, you will only be taxed on $60

---

140 Bregman, *Utopia for Realists*, 199.
141 "Ultra-Millionaire Tax," Warren Campaign.

- $50 = $10 million). The rate would be 2 percent per year on that $10 million, leaving the rest of their money alone. (Warren calls this program the "Ultra-Millionaire Tax," but I think it's a bad name. It will get shortened to the millionaire tax, and then people will think it could affect them. Billionaire Tax actually gets at the heart of the matter. Fat Cat Tax could be fun as well.)

Let's break down what this means:

- People can still get pretty damn wealthy.

    - Quick, think of someone who makes a lot of money! Chances are, you thought of an athlete, actor, or musician. Just for fun, let's take one of the Kardashians: Kendall Jenner is the highest-paid model in the world, with a net worth of $45 million as of 2020.[142] Not bad, right? Still won't get hit by the wealth tax. For another random example, let's do Cardi B. One of the most famous people on the planet still won't get taxed because she only has $30 million.[143] Maybe you're sitting around thinking, "Cardi B sucks, my mixtape is going to blow up," in which case, good for you, dude! It probably won't happen, but even if you hit #1 on the Billboard charts a few times over, you still probably won't make enough for the wealth tax. Drop those tunes without fear.

    - The average person ends up making between one and three million dollars over the course of their

---

142 Day, "Kardashian-Jenner Family's Net Worth."
143 "Cardi B Net Worth," *Celebrity Net Worth*.

career (e.g., if you made the median income of $65,000 for forty-five years and paid no taxes, you would make just under $3 million), but still have to spend money to survive. Even if you had your entire life savings up front, you wouldn't get taxed.

- Seriously, think about how much money $50 million is. If someone gave you $100,000 right now, you'd probably call that a life-changing amount of money. You'd still be $49,900,000 away from being taxed.

- You can reward people for innovation without enabling a system where people have almost ludicrous amounts of money. If Jeff Bezos spent 99.5 percent of his money, he would still have a Billion Dollars.

- Money Still Makes Money

  - A wealth tax won't stop the ultrawealthy from getting richer. It'll just slow the rate at which they get richer than everyone else. The easiest retirement advice you can get is "Put your money in the S&P 500." Over the course of its existence, the S&P 500 has grown about 10 percent a year. Even with a 2 percent tax, a person taking the absolute most passive approach to investing will still get 8 percent richer every year without working.

  - Piketty's work showed that the annual economic growth rate over the last two hundred years averaged around 2 percent a year, while the historic rate of return on capital was 4–5 percent. Let's be generous and use the low end. If you had $1,000 and received a 2 percent return every year for 100 years, you would have $7,244.65. If you had $1,000 and received a 4 percent return every year for 100 years, you would have $50,504.95. Compound interest is a crazy thing.

SO WHAT?

Maybe you're one of those people who doesn't find it strange that billionaires haven't decided to end homelessness or world hunger, or at least fund our school systems enough that teachers don't have to buy their own supplies. But having this much wealth concentrated into the hands of only a few hundred people is dangerous.

Maybe you're thinking to yourself right now, "If I defend the Koch brothers online, maybe, he'll give me some of his money," like a middle schooler waiting for Harry Styles to find her fan fiction and sweep her off her feet. These are for you.

DANGEROUS FOR DEMOCRACY:
Unfortunately, money matters in politics. It's complicated, but we have Citizens United most recently to thank, which equated the use of money to free speech.

Think back to Mike Bloomberg. Had he been slightly more charismatic than a wet paper bag, he had a real chance to buy his way into the presidency. Doesn't that strike you as concerning?

We create the system that we want. Do you want a political system where only the wealthy have a voice in politics?

Take another example, maybe a billionaire who doesn't want the limelight. When you stand to save hundreds of millions or even billions of dollars, donating millions of dollars to politicians is just good financial sense. It goes against the idea of one person, one vote.

DANGEROUS FOR SOCIETY:
It's already possible for the ultrawealthy to buy up all the good shit. Just look at Larry Ellison buying an entire Hawaiian island or Mark Zuckerberg buying holy land in Kawaii. The only reason some of us still have a beach to go to is that Elon Musk doesn't want to step foot in Myrtle Beach.

But what does this look like in the coming age of automation? There's going to come a point in the near future where a line of code or a robot will be able to do any job better than a human. Machines will be better coders than us, machines will be better truck drivers than us, and machines will be better corn harvesters. It's also going to be significantly more profitable to hire them because they don't eat or sleep, and you don't need to pay them.

There's a chance this could be the solution to all of humanity's problems. Maybe we'll have a Star Trek like post-scarcity society, where no one needs to work, and everyone can spend their life enjoying the company of family and friends.

On the other hand, what if it goes poorly? America is supposed to be the land of opportunity, but what happens when no single person can hope to find a niche to earn a living that isn't occupied by the army of Bezos Bots?

Without jobs, how will people earn a living? Without a middle and lower class buying their products, what society will the billionaires rule over?

CHAPTER 9

WHAT'S THE WORST THAT COULD HAPPEN?

Andrew Mellon was one of the last of the robber barons. Born to the wealthy Mellon family in Pennsylvania, he inherited the family banking business. In addition to the ninety-nine banks he controlled, he "had interests in coal, steel, chemicals, oil, sleeping cars, railroads, building construction, utilities, magnesium, and airplanes."[144] In the 1800s, aluminum was twice as valuable as gold. His company, Alcoa, grew from the late 1800s to eventually own 100 percent of the aluminum market in the period between the World Wars when the metal was used in everything from cars to planes and cooking utensils. Alcoa used its uniquely powerful monopoly position to crush its enemies and threaten its customers.[145]

When Mellon got bored, he loaned Warren Harding's presidential campaign 1.5 million in 1920 dollars to become

---

144 Stoller, *Goliath*, 35–37

145 Ibid, 130-134.

Secretary of the Treasury.[146] He kept this position during Harding's administration, through Coolidge's, and then to Hoover's, with one senator quipping, "three presidents served under him."[147] Through his position as Secretary of the Treasury, he set tax policy and government debt policy and became chairman of the Federal Reserve, and under his rule, the Wall Street Journal remarked that "Never before, here or anywhere else, has a government been so completely fused with business."[148]

This monopolist wielded his political power to reverse the trust-busting trend of the previous decades by essentially limiting all anti-monopoly government action, enriched himself and other monopolists by giving huge companies massive tax refunds, and even used the precursor of the IRS to investigate senators who got in his way.[149]

Through his business power, Mellon turned coal country Pennsylvania into "a system of despotic tyranny reminiscent of Czar-ridden Siberia at its worst," featuring "police brutality and industrial slavery." There were "thousands of women and children literally starving to death . . . [and] hundreds of destitute families living in crudely constructed bare-board shacks" because Mellon's coal companies evicted them from their homes.[150]

---

146 Ibid, 34.
147 Ibid, 35.
148 Ibid, 39-43.
149 Ibid, 40.
150 Ibid, 45.

His brother, Richard Mellon, admitted to the Senate that you couldn't run a mine without machine guns aimed at the miners to keep them in line and from organizing.[151] Andrew Mellon may have been unique in his political power but not in his business tactics. When 365,000 workers went on strike against US Steel to form a union, the company employed tens of thousands of private security guards, killing twenty and going so far as to declare martial law in Gary, Indiana.[152]

In retrospect, Mellon's fall from grace seems almost miraculous. Mellon resigned in 1931 when he faced impeachment from his position because of his corruption.[153] Following the Wall Street crash, the government attempted to hold the bankers responsible accountable, Mellon included. He was at first acquitted before the precursor to the IRS took action to hold him for avoiding taxes through complex financial schemes. At first, things looked pretty good for him, as he had established the Board of Tax Appeals where he was being tried and filled it with lackeys. He even tried to donate artwork and build the National Gallery to build goodwill, but his shady practices were impossible to avoid. He lost the case but died soon after, and his estate settled with the government.[154]

COULDN'T HAVE HAPPENED TO A NICER GUY

Government corruption resulting in someone resigning and later facing major fines was wild for me to hear about. But

---

151 Ibid, 46.
152 Ibid, 31.
153 Ibid, 78.
154 Ibid, 109-117.

the craziest part of the story, however, was that Andrew Mellon fucking loved Benito Mussolini. He visited the original Fascist dictator in office and glowingly spoke of how efficient Italy was under Fascist rule. He even talked up fascism while campaigning for Republican nominee Herbert Hoover, contrasting how efficient it was versus communism.[155]

Crazier still, he wasn't alone! Businessmen loved fascism. Bankers loaned Mussolini loads, and the chairman of US Steel told Americans to "learn something by the movement which has taken place in Italy."[156] While not a businessman, the president of Columbia University "told his freshman class that totalitarian dictatorships were putting forward 'men of far greater intelligence, far stronger character, and far more courage than the system of elections.'"[157]

This wasn't limited to Italian fascism. Tons of American money poured into fascist Germany in the '30s—everyone from the DuPonts, to General Motors, to J.P. Morgan.[158] Hitler repaid the investors pouring money into his country by dissolving unions, then throwing Communists in jail, and later building concentration camps.

I'm not telling you this to kick people who have been dead for decades. It's to underline the fact that America had its flirtation with fascism, lead in part by business leaders.

---

155 Ibid, 49.
156 Ibid, 48.
157 Ibid, 68.
158 Pauwels, "Profits 'Über Alles!'" 203.

The word gets thrown around a lot, and people often use it willy-nilly. Before we move on, let's look at how Franklin Delano Roosevelt described it just before World War II:

> "The liberty of a democracy is not safe if the people tolerate the growth of private power to a point where it becomes stronger than their democratic state itself. That, in its essence, is Fascism—ownership of government by an individual, by a group, or by any other controlling private power."[159]

DEMOCRACY AT RISK

Was 2020 really the election of a lifetime? Was the fate of our democracy truly on the line there, or is the threat of fascism only present when you're running against that one guy?

Maybe I bought into the bluff, but I do think that Pandora's Box has been opened, and it's up to the left to be the adults in the room and prevent it from happening again. Now that power-hungry politicians know checks and balances only work when your own party is willing to check your power, more will attempt to try it, and it won't just be those who luck their way into the presidency to try and bail themselves out of debt.

Before 1954, experts thought that running a mile in under four minutes was physically impossible. Then Roger Bannister ran it in 3:59:4, shattering our expectations of what was possible. A month and a half later, someone beat Bannister's

---

159 Roosevelt, "Message to Congress on Curbing Monopolies."

record. One race the next year had three runners break the so-called impossible barrier that people had been trying to break sincerely since 1886. Over a thousand athletes have passed this threshold, in large part due to the knowledge that their goal is possible.[160]

For the same reason, I'm sure Senator Hawley and other ghouls sat around on January 6th watching the insurrection, licking their chops.

Democracy is not the default option when it comes to government. It's really hard to maintain. For much of America's history, it was only a democracy if you were a rich white man. Democracy as a concept hasn't been popular for all of our history. A 1928 US Army training manual even concluded that democracy resulted in "demagoguism, license, agitation, discontent, anarchy."[161]

We're seeing democracy erode in front of our eyes, like how people of color are being stripped of their right to vote again. In 2013, the Supreme Court ruled a major part of the Voting Rights Act of 1965 unconstitutional. While the Voting Rights Act legally prevented people from being barred from voting due to the color of their skin, the 2013 ruling made it almost impossible for the government to both determine if someone is being prevented from voting due to that fact and taking action on that fact.[162] One in five polling places in Arizona were closed between 2013 and 2019, and one in

---

160 Taylor, "Breaking the Four-Minute Mile."
161 Stoller, *Goliath*, 29.
162 Howe, "Details on Shelby County v. Holder."

ten polling places in Texas was closed over the same period. Many counties in Georgia only have one polling place now. All told, 1,200 polling places were closed over that period, predominantly in states with histories of racial discrimination. Some of those states have also added photo ID laws or other restrictions with controversial histories.[163] Racism at the polls is still alive and well.

If this was the election to save our democracy, now is the time to put some measures in place to, you know, save our democracy. Put some laws on the books because no matter how many thoughts and prayers I send, Mitch McConnell is still walking around.

WHOA, EASY WITH THE F-WORD!

Robert Paxton, one of the definitive historians on the subject of fascism, defines the term pretty broadly: "a popular movement against the Left and against liberal individualism."[164] Fascism in one place can look very different from fascism in another. Just think about how America as a republic looks pretty different from Ancient Rome as a republic, or Soviet Poland looked very different from communist Cuba.

Fascism in America, too, would look very different from anything else beforehand. Sure, we can look back at what became fascism somewhat easily. But what could we expect looking forward?

---

163 Sullivan, "Southern US States."
164 Paxton, *The Anatomy of Fascism*, 20.

"The language and symbols of an authentic American fascism would, of course, have little to do with the original European models. They would have to be as familiar and reassuring to loyal Americans as the language and symbols of the original fascisms were familiar and reassuring to many Italians and Germans, as Orwell suggested. Hitler and Mussolini, after all, had not tried to seem exotic to their fellow citizens. **No swastikas in an American fascism, but Stars and Stripes (or Stars and Bars) and Christian crosses. No fascist salute, but mass recitations of the pledge of allegiance.** These symbols contain no whiff of fascism in themselves, of course, but **an American fascism would transform them into obligatory litmus tests for detecting the internal enemy.** Around such reassuring language and symbols in the event of some redoubtable setback to national prestige, Americans might support an enterprise of forcible national regeneration, unification, and purification. **Its targets would be the First Amendment, separation of Church and State (creches on the lawns, prayers in schools), efforts to place control on gun ownership, desecrations of the flag, unassimilated minorities,** artistic license, dissident and unusual behavior of all sorts that could be labeled antinational or decadent." (emphasis mine)

—ROBERT PAXTON

YouTuber Cody Johnston makes the point that American fascism would have familiar things like baseball caps with slogans about returning America to Greatness and might spark outrage about someone in public refusing to stand for the national anthem.[165] I'll leave it to you to ponder where gun control or efforts to turn American into a Christian nation would come into play.

A lot of the right's current behavior doesn't seem like guided ideology so much as reactionary movements against the left. Newt Gingrich, former Speaker of the House who helped shape the Republican party we know today, described Trump as "not essentially a conservative. Trump is an anti-liberal."[166] That's the kind of shit that makes me pause. (If you want a super brief rundown on the other shit that makes me pause, I highly recommend the video "Let's Talk about Trump's Accomplishments" by Beau of the Fifth Column on YouTube. It's six and a half minutes and worth your time.)

I don't think that Andrew Mellon, or any of the other business tycoons of the early twentieth century, was enthusiastic about Mussolini or Hitler because of deep hatred for minorities or knowledge about what the movement would become. I think they smelled an opportunity for themselves and liked any system that would allow them to keep making millions and millions on the backs of laborers. In the same way, I don't think that today's billionaires are encouraging further deregulation for any ideology other than the love of seeing their net worths creep higher and higher. Playing off hatred on the right is just an easy tactic to keep everyone else divided. However, we do have the benefit of knowing what stoking

---

165 Some More News, "Trumpism Is Just a Synonym for Fascism."
166 Venkataramanan, "Trump Is the 'Most Effective Uprooter.'"

nationalism and race-baiting in the pursuit of concentrated power can lead to.

But what if we cut out nationalism and racism?

Fine. Let's stop using the F-word. Even if you take out the nationalism and racism, you're still left with an oligarchy. Wealth and political power are concentrating at the top, and it's getting worse every year. As former Secretary of Labor Robert Reich put it, "Forget politics as you've come to see it, as electoral contests between Democrats and Republicans. Think power. The underlying contest is between a small minority who have gained power over the system and the vast majority who have little or none."[167] Oligarchy is rule by the few for their own sake. The rest of us are left in the dust.

America has seen what has oligarchy looked like in the past. It looked like Andrew Mellon or other monopolists with so much power that their employees were forced to live in shacks or work in mines with machine guns pointed at them. Oligarchy in the future would probably look slightly different. Maybe it would look like newspapers being pushed out of business by the thousands as all of the world's advertising revenue is concentrated between two companies. Maybe it would look like one large employer pushing out any small retailer and enforcing such strict metrics that employees take to peeing in bottles on the job to increase productivity.

Deregulation has led to the concentration of wealth and power. With that new power, the lucky few are able to rig the system

---

167 Reich, *The System: Who Rigged It, How We Fix It*, 7.

for more deregulation, and the cycle continues. Whether you think the future is oligarchy or fascism, it doesn't bode well for democracy.

That is unless we take it back. We've beaten it before. Programs like the New Deal put prosperity within reach for common people who were able to lead happy, fulfilling lives. Decades of concentrated wealth and power were beaten by a virtuous cycle. The government started to work for the people, and the people started to believe in the government again. Rather than running on cultural issues of the day like the prohibition of alcohol or what to do with the KKK, Democrats began having real policies that gave people better lives in material ways. We don't have a historical playbook here, but we've done it before. Let's do it again.

Democracy is founded on the idea that people are equal and deserve a say in how things are run. It's time to start acting like we believe it.

CHAPTER 10

PROGRESSIVES AS THE SOLUTION

Jon Stewart interviewed Nancy Pelosi on the Daily Show in 2014, when he still hosted the show, and she was the House Minority Leader. Pelosi made the agreeable claim that we "must reduce the role of money in politics."[168] Excellent idea! One problem: Nancy Pelosi had just raised $30 million for her political action committee, a group that advertises on her behalf. If the problem in politics is corruption because of money, wouldn't fundraising leave her vulnerable to corruption?

Nope! It turns out she's incorruptible, and it's only political opponents who are open to the fraudulent forces of money. Just knowing that money corrupts makes you immune to its effects. The two then disagreed about whether or not the political system was corrupt, with Pelosi arguing that "There is corruption in the system, but the system isn't corrupt," and

---

168 *The Daily Show with Jon Stewart*, "Nancy Pelosi Extended Interview."

Stewart saying that "The system has been utterly overrun by moneyed interests," as even Democrats take money from energy companies and Wall Street. After all, "To suggest that one party has a problem with moneyed interest and the other doesn't is a somewhat unfair characterization."[169] For what it's worth, I side with Stewart.

Let's call it like it is for a second: A fair amount of politicians out there don't give a shit about you. The preferences of average citizens have little to no impact on policy because business interests and the wealthy are overrepresented.[170] Wealthy Americans have different policy preferences than the rest of us. Even nominally liberal wealthy people tend to hold really conservative viewpoints when it comes to financial policy, likely because they have the most to lose.[171]

This probably isn't anything surprising. After all, only 20 percent of Americans trust their government to do the right thing.[172] That's something you can't brush away by blaming QAnon, Russian interference, or any other recent phenomena.

The common refrain of people who don't vote is that "It simply doesn't matter who I vote for. They're both for the same things." To be fair to these people, they have a point. I don't agree, but they have a point. The entire political system has shifted so far right that there aren't huge economic differences between the two. Biden wants to raise the top marginal tax rate to 39.6 percent

---

169 Ibid.

170 Gilens and Page, "Testing Theories of American Politics."

171 Page, Bartels, and Seawright, "Democracy & Policy Preferences."

172 " Americans' Views of Government," *Pew Research.*

from 37 percent—a step in the right direction, but a drop in the bucket.[173] Now consider that 70 years ago, the top marginal tax rate under Eisenhower, a Republican, averaged 81 percent.[174]

For a bigger picture perspective, consider the 2008 financial collapse. If you're Barack Obama and America has a banking collapse due to mortgages, the two parties at risk are the bank and the person who might lose their home. Someone has to pay for what's about to happen. Under his Trouble Asset Relief Program, the main bailout package, people weren't allowed to write off their mortgages, so nine million people suffered foreclosures, and "America's middle class lost between $5 and $7 trillion in wealth."[175] If I didn't know who lead the Wall Street bailout, I wouldn't be able to tell you which party did it, especially when you line it up next to Trump's coronavirus response package.

Both Democrats and Republicans are funded by corporate interests. In the 2016 election, Wall Street spent thirty-four times as much money as unions or public interest groups, and that money went to both parties.[176]

People can't really tell the difference between, say, a 37 percent tax rate and a 39.6 percent tax rate. When politicians refuse to differentiate themselves on economic issues, all they're left with is cultural issues. If they won't materially make people's lives better, they can only make voters feel like part of a team. Otherwise, the only option is apathy.

---

173 Scott, "Explaining Biden's Tax Plan."
174 Saez and Zucman, *Triumph of Injustice*, 35.
175 Stoller, *Goliath*, 436.
176 Reich, *The System*, 56.

WHO CAN PAY?

Have you ever heard the saying about Facebook and other companies that if you don't pay for a service, you're the product, not the customer? That is to say, you don't pay for Facebook because their business model is to sell your attention and your data to companies who buy advertising space.

Voting for corporatist Democrats (or Republicans) is a lot like that. Identity issues are easy. They can support those nominally left-leaning cultural issues but work in favor of big corporate interests who fund their campaigns and trade in cultural issues for votes, then swap pro-business legislation for cash in the form of campaign donations. Citizens' votes are the raw materials that get turned into politicians' voting records, consumed by the ultimate customer: the corporation.

Voters saw this plain as day with Hillary Clinton's high-priced public speaking fees. Someone else was paying her high prices, and whoever it was likely to get what they wanted. Frankly, they were right. It was pretty sketchy. Unfortunately, the alternative was someone willing to sell his public policy decisions for even cheaper and to worse people. At a campaign rally, Trump even bragged about it: "Saudi Arabia, I get along with all of them. They buy apartments from me. They spend $40 million, $50 million. . . . Am I supposed to dislike them? I like them very much."[177] It turns out if you're open about being corrupt, people don't give a shit.

Politicians and the media threw a fit over Russian interference in the 2016 election. To be clear, it happened, it was real,

---

177 Mangan, "Trump: Financial Interests in Saudi Arabia."

and it's a bad thing. But why do we willingly accept the idea of American corporate interference in our elections? When corporations give money to other candidates hoping to affect the outcomes of elections and gain influence, it's completely legal. Sure, we make a small distinction of Americans vs. Russians influencing our politicians, but the main difference is that both parties are guilty of one of these issues. Democrats know they don't have the superiority here, so they harped on a peripheral issue rather than policies that affect voters' lives.

People aren't stupid. They know that this happens.

Democrats attempt to play the moral superiority card, and many people who aren't already in the party simply don't buy it. Sure, you can make the point that the party that has white supremacists in the mix has less moral ground, but if someone doesn't know that already, they won't know now. If only there were a type of people who were interested in politics for the sake of doing the right thing, regardless of how it affects their careers or paychecks.

PROGRESSIVES: CURE FOR THE COMMON CANDIDATE

If your audience thinks you don't give a shit about them, your options are to either A) make it so you don't need an audience or B) start to give a shit about them. Unfortunately, the electoral college is working to the right's advantage here, so A is out of the option. It looks like the only long-term solution for electability is to start giving a shit about people.

The right has a monopoly on the idea that "The government doesn't work for people. Let's get rid of it." The best counter to that isn't gaslighting Americans, especially when they've seen how much the government works to support large corporations rather than them. The best counter to that is, "The government doesn't work for people. Let's make it work for people."

Thus far, it seems that the Democratic party is content to campaign on issues that could help people and then not deliver. If that's the case, then it's time for voters to consider an alternative to the traditional candidates. One of the most important trends of the 2018 and 2020 elections has been seeing progressive outsiders with a shot for winning seats. When Alexandria Ocasio-Cortez ran, she was a bartender running against a ten-term incumbent, one of the most powerful party members who had been leading her race by 36 percentage points.[178] Cori Bush ousted someone who had held the seat since 2001.[179] Marie Newman won a race for a House seat that had been held by a father and then his son since 1983.[180]

Seeing a former bartender and a community organizer win elections should give us all hope because we know they believe in their issues. When someone who used to work for tips says she's fighting to raise the minimum wage, I believe her because she has lived the alternative. When a former nurse advocates for Medicare for All, I see someone who has skin in the game.

Grassroots elections show you that person isn't beholden to special interests. They earned their seats by listening to their

---

178 Goldmacher, "An Upset in the Making."
179 Yancey-Bragg and Cummings, "Cori Bush."
180 O'Connell, "Marie Newman's Victory."

constituents, and they should have the sense to keep doing so. It's much harder to corrupt someone who truly believes in what they're pushing for.

Republicans have the sense to do what their constituents want, even when it's ridiculous. Sixty-eight percent of Republican voters had concerns about whether or not the election was rigged.[181] One hundred and six Republican representatives supported a lawsuit to overturn the election, even though they knew it wasn't.[182] After all, that same election is how those Republicans got their seats!

Contrast that with the Georgia senate races. Then President-elect Biden said that $2,000 "will go out the door immediately" if the Georgia senate seats flipped for the Democrats.[183] After those seats flipped, the promise became $1,400 checks.

This isn't to naively complain about broken promises by a politician. This is to say that when your competition is actually working on their promises, you're at a competitive disadvantage if you don't do the same thing. Incumbents need to recognize that if they don't change their behavior, they will be changed.

Why is this exclusive to progressives? When you run a campaign based on the idea that corporate interests are making life worse for average people, those corporate interests aren't very likely to give you money. When you

---

181 Castronuovo, "Half of Republicans."
182 Solender, "106 House Republicans."
183 Duffy, "Biden Tells Georgia Voters."

say that insurance companies are profiting off of keeping people from getting health care, you aren't likely to raise money from insurance companies.

On the other hand, if people believe that you are actually working on their behalf, they are more likely to care about your campaign. Once you burn bridges with Big Pharma or Big Insurance, you're only really left with Big Poor. Take Bernie's campaign, for example. Before Super Tuesday, his campaign raised $167 million from 8.7 million contributions.[184] That means the average donation was just under $20. It's a similar story for Alexandria Ocasio-Cortez, who gets 80 percent of her funds from small contributions.[185]

Other people are free to steal this idea. If the only sources of campaign power are popular will and corporate money, you have to double down on one. Republicans have the advantage that taking corporate money fits within their worldview. If you're fundamentalist for the market, taking corporate money is kosher. When your strategy is to make people believe that the government works for them, on the other hand, you have to work for them, and corporate money will get in the way. I'm sure in some world it's possible that someone could take the money and run, opting to work for the rest of us, but I'm not holding my breath.

But what about after the campaign, when they're in office? How do you stay committed to working for your constituents? I'd like to look for inspiration from a surprising place.

---

184 Marans and Miller, "Bernie Sanders Campaign."
185 "Rep. Ocasio-Cortez," OpenSecrets.

WHATEVER HAPPENED TO THE TEA PARTY?

Donald Trump gets a lot of credit for pulling off an inter-party coup that few in the political establishment saw coming. You can't pretend that his winning the Republican nomination wasn't an upset, and you really can't pretend his winning the election was expected from the get-go. But there was another unexpected turnover a few years before that could have given us a hint of what was to come but gets brushed over in all of the coverage on Trump.

In February 2009, a trader named Rick Santelli ranted on CNBC from the floor of the Chicago Mercantile Exchange. This man was heated and said that "the government was promoting bad behavior" and "subsidiz[ing] the losers' mortgages." When he spoke the words, "We're thinking of having a Chicago Tea Party in July. All you capitalists that want to show up to Lake Michigan, I'm going to start organizing," the people around him cheered and whistled.[186]

Prophetically, the finance analyst following that tough act stated, "Well, clearly we're going to debate the moral issues on what the government is and isn't doing for years to come."[187]

Santelli's rant went viral and became a rallying cry for a network of conservatives on the internet who had been posting and networking the entire preceding year. Spark meets kindling. By April, over 600 Tea Party protests and events drove almost 600,000 attendants.[188]

---

186 The Heritage Foundation, "CNBC's Rick Santelli's Chicago Tea Party."
187 Ibid.
188 Rauch, "Group Think."

The Tea Party started as a decentralized group of people ranting to each other on forums. By October of 2010, 35 percent of likely voters considered themselves supporters of the Tea Party.[189] In 2013, 65 percent of Republicans viewed the Tea Party favorably.[190] For comparison, 7 percent of Americans considered themselves libertarians, while another 7 percent considered themselves in the same year.[191]

The Tea Party tried to label itself as against the reach of the so-called "big government" as an offshoot of libertarianism. The timing of its creation, immediately after the political campaign for the Affordable Care Act, could be interpreted as proof of this fact. The government tries to act, and then there's a movement that works to hogtie the government's ability to act. Action, reaction.

Tea Partiers won 32 percent of their races in 2010, but a fair number ran in races that were lost causes from the start (i.e., a Republican running in a deeply blue race would likely lose regardless of whether or not they were a Tea Partier). Those who ran in competitive races won at about the same rate as traditional Republicans.[192]

By 2012, "the face of the Tea Party caucus in Washington" was chosen as the vice-presidential candidate on the GOP ticket. By having Paul Ryan front and center, the Tea Party went from a "fringe of the conservative coalition" to "the

---

189 Weisman, "GOP in Lead in Final Lap."

190 Bowman and Marisco, "As the Tea Party Turns Five."

191 Goodman, "Libertarians by the Numbers."

192 Nyhan, "Beware Context-Free Election Analysis."

core of the modern Republican Party."[193] The next year, freshman Senator Ted Cruz, elected largely with Tea Party support, lead a charge to shut down the government for two weeks during Obamacare negotiations.[194] For a group that fundamentally doesn't believe in the power of the government, furloughing 800,000 government employees during the then-second longest shutdown in history represented a serious show of political power.

The real upset came two years later. Tea Party members in the House of Representatives formed the Freedom Caucus in early 2015 and in July filed a motion to vacate the House chair. It's an obscure rule that had only been used once before in history, more than a hundred years prior, and the Tea Party was attempting to force out the Republican Speaker of the House (the most powerful seat), John Boehner.[195] The motion didn't proceed for wonky technical reasons, but Boehner stepped down two months later, eventually replaced by Tea Partier Paul Ryan.

Within five years, Tea Partiers had had a run at the executive office, pushed out one of the most powerful Republicans, and replaced him with one of their own. They even made him cry on camera![196]

WHY AM I TELLING YOU THIS?
Outsider groups have strength if they fight for their constituents.

---

193 Shear, "Ryan Brings the Tea Party to the Ticket."
194 Fahrenthold and Zezima, "For Ted Cruz."
195 Berman, "Boehner Says No Thanks."
196 Siddiqui, Jacobs, and McCarthy, "John Boehner to Resign."

Let's separate the strategy from the movement for a second here (in case I haven't been clear, race-baiting and shutting down the government isn't my idea of a good time).

The Tea Party fought like hell for their issues. They read the signs, saw that huge numbers of people were sympathetic to the cause, and then worked their asses off no matter how stupid they looked. Do you think Ted Cruz didn't know that he looked fucking crazy?

Tea Partiers in the House formed a voting bloc, or caucus called the Freedom Caucus. As the members of the Freedom Caucus were coming up with a name, one of the choices was "The Reasonable Nutjob Caucus."[197] (This isn't a joke. Imagine my surprise researching a group of Don Quixotes only to find out that they came up with a better gag than I could).

The Freedom Caucus started with nine members and did the math. They needed twenty more members of their group to get the negotiating power to break a Republican majority in the house. They found twenty-five. Eventually, that number swelled to its current size of forty-eight. Founding member Mick Mulvaney said, "Ever since I got here, in 2010, the one thing they said is you could never ever, ever, ever vote against a rule. And what we told the guys we recruited into the Freedom Caucus was that you have to be able to do it."[198]

Tea Partiers found obscure strategies to force the party's hands and even shut down the government. They weren't

---

197 Lizza, "The War Inside the Republican Party."
198 Ibid.

constrained by the idea of political civility or of following traditional processes. Not being the majority forces you to get creative. Rather than being embarrassed by the extremity of their constituents' views, they leaned into them, and the constituents rewarded them with votes. For mainstream party members, this has the added benefit of having someone else catch flack for your actions. It's not all Republicans that are like this—just the Jim Jordans.

But whatever happened to the Tea Party?

You know in Scooby Doo when the Gang is running around in circles looking for a monster and ask for directions from a ten-foot-tall gentleman wearing the same blood-stained clothes except this guy has a mustache? Same thing.

Take the Freedom Caucus, for example, which is still largely led by former Tea Partiers. But beyond that, much of the Tea Party viewpoint and strategy is part of the Republican platform. Railing against the Affordable Care Act and immigrants and a childlike insistence on removing any and all regulations are proudly center stage. They've shed the name and put on a pair of glasses, but they're still the same monster.

Donald Trump is the logical conclusion to the Tea Party saga. Trump courted Tea Party voters within two months of his campaign announcement (just a month after they pushed Boehner out), laying praise like "the Tea Party are incredible people [. . .] who work hard for their people and they get beat up all the time by the media."[199] While he started

---

199 Lee, "Donald Trump Courts Tea Party."

his campaign with a fringe group of Tea Party support, his presidency maintained an in-party approval rating in the 80s and 90s for four years.[200] Tea Party politics are simply mainstream Republican politics.

No one really calls them the Tea Party anymore. The label served its use because there was a new, orange-tinted metric to measure yourself by. Reporters focused their pieces on Trump because he was a topic that sells. Journalism is a product, and you have to market your product so customers would actually buy it. No one was reading pieces about the Tea Party, but people would read Trump news because they hated it. People would also read Trump news because they loved it.

Same thing with politicians. The Tea Party label wasn't getting the votes, so they switched to a new label that meant the same thing.

WHY ARE YOU TELLING ME THIS?
Rick Santelli's rant is given credit for lighting the spark that set off the Tea Party organizing movement. But before the rant and before the protests that drew thousands of people, loads of right-wing bloggers were writing about their dissatisfaction and creating the network of people that the movement needed to take off.

Ironically, one blogger who was credited with helping to start the movement found inspiration on the other side of the aisle. "Unlike the melodramatic lefties, I do not want to get arrested.

---

200 Gallup, "Presidential Approval Ratings—Trump."

I do, however, want to take a page from their playbook and be loud, obnoxious, and in their faces," Keli Carender said.[201]

Carender said this in early 2010, before the elections of Ted Cruz, Mick Mulvaney, and other Tea Party-associated freshmen who would take the dissatisfaction of their constituents and turn it into policy, but we should keep in mind that grassroots organizing is a traditional strength of the left.

The progressive wing is uniquely suited to take advantage of this strategy: Organize in favor of issues and then fight like hell for them. In fact, it might be the only strategy that could work. All they need is a spark.

Trying to push established politicians left has proven itself to be difficult. If someone is already in office, what leverage do you have over them? They already have their goal of being in office, and the advantage of being an incumbent in seat is one of the greatest advantages in politics. (Presidents in office, for example, are much more likely to win than someone running for the first time.) Joe Biden was pushed left on climate policy in order to bring Sanders' supporters into his camp before the election. Now that he has their votes, it's unlikely that he will take on more of their positions out of the goodness of his heart.

Furthermore, someone who is already in office is just going to spend more of their time being surrounded by well-financed lobbyists than someone running for the first time on a progressive ticket. Democrats campaigned for the Georgia senate

---

201 McGrath, "The Movement."

seats by promising $2,000 checks. After these elections, these promises suddenly turned into $1,400 checks for fewer people. That's a shift, right. A shift left would have looked like giving money to more people who were cut out for arbitrary reasons or giving bigger checks to recognize that many people have been out of work for a year.

(Some might counter that Massachusetts Senator Ed Markey shifted to the left by coauthoring the Green New Deal along with Alexandria Ocasio-Cortez. While this is a fair point, Markey had served as the Chairman of the Select Committee on Energy Independence and Global Warming in the House while it existed a decade before the Green New Deal.[202] I think it's safe to say that he's been somewhat consistent on this issue.)

We've seen that the Democratic party won't willingly shift to the left on issues like a $15 minimum wage, for example. To make a long story short, some Democrats tried to include it is as part of Biden's relief package, but it was axed by senators like Joe Manchin, the conservative Democrat from West Virginia, ostensibly because of wonky reasons no one gives a shit about. It's the old "you're lucky my friends held me back so I couldn't fight you" technique.

So, if there's an issue that A) progressive voters care about, B) progressive congressmen theoretically care about, and C) will tangibly make people's lives better, what's a progressive to do? Think back to our frenemy Mick Mulvaney for a second, who was told he could never ever, ever, ever vote against a

---

202 "About Ed," Markey Campaign.

rule and decided to recruit other people to help him vote against that rule and ended up replacing one of the heads of the party. They didn't have more political clout than any other freshmen congressmen until they showed that they meant business.

In negotiations, this is called the Best Alternative to a Negotiated Agreement. Basically, one of the most efficient ways to get what you want is to know that your co-negotiator doesn't have an alternative to working with you. Democrats knew that they needed to pass, say, the COVID relief bill and send out those checks. They campaigned on it! It could be their signature achievement. Put simply, party leadership really needs it to go through for the sake of their careers. Their best alternative is looking like losers and getting slaughtered in the midterms.

If progressives want to help people, they need to have some fucking balls.

Power comes from exercising power. John Boehner didn't step down because he saw the light; he saw that he was up against a group of people who were willing to fight for what their constituents believed in and would win reelection to do so. It's the same tactic, but instead of serving as an ego trip for some rich dudes, it would improve the lives of millions of Americans.

No one's going to be mad that they didn't do it the orthodox way. They're just going to be happy that they can afford the rent for a month. If you think this won't work, consider the fact that Joe Manchin will be doing this schtick for as long as the Senate is evenly split, and he's just one guy. We've already seen him dictate what Democrats do in the Senate. Now imagine harnessing that effort to get people living wages or health care. The party is already going to throw progressives under the bus. We may as well get something done before that happens.

Beyond that, centrist Democrats need progressives to do it for the sake of their party. Sometimes the only way you can break a bad habit is to have somebody else step in. It's hard to decide one day to turn your back on the corporate donors who helped get you in office in the first place. Not impossible, but certainly very hard. When the problem is that your voters don't think you represent their interests, you're at risk of losing those voters permanently. Republicans have shown that they're willing to play dirty to stay in power, and failing to turn out voters could allow them to set new rules for the foreseeable future.

Democrats are setting themselves up for a bad losing streak. Nothing would make me happier than for the Ghost of Voters Past, Present, and Future to visit Joe Biden on Christmas Eve and show him the error of his ways. But if that doesn't happen, we need a progressive voting bloc to stand up for all of us.

NO MONOPOLY ON PROGRESS

Here's a crazy thought to end the chapter: Republicans can be progressives, too.

Theodore Roosevelt, one of the most popular presidents in history, defined himself as a Republican progressive. The "speak softly and carry a big stick" guy used that stick to fight for average Americans by going after the monopolies of his time and breaking up big banks like J.P. Morgan. Progressivism isn't a left/right issue. All you have to do to be a progressive is believe we can head toward a better society by giving more power to the people—and then fighting for it.

Much of this book has been about longer-term strategies for the Democratic party. That's not because I think Democrats are inherently good, or Republicans are inherently, uh, the opposite. It's because the last few years have made it clear that Republicans don't care about fighting inequality or keeping us all healthy. They might even think inequality is a good thing.

Politics is a team sport. That being said, we can make a choice to stop having the only teams be Republican or Democrat. Republicans aren't precluded from having progressive goals. Republicans have a long history of supporting progressive issues. Even Richard Nixon almost passed through an early form of Universal Basic Income.

I'm rooting for whichever team wants to work to reduce inequality and steward the environment, but that can change. Currently, the only people on that team are Democrats, but that can change. Biden was asked if he was serious about bipartisanship within days of being in office, but I can't for the life of me find someone who asked the same question of Trump. These attempts to meet the right in the middle are a large part of how our politics have gone so far to the right.

In an ideal world, you vote on what someone believes, not their party. I don't believe that the problem is we won't meet with Republican progressives. I think the problem is that Republican progressives can't exist in the Republican party as it currently exists.

With that being said, let me be the first to extend an olive branch to any potential Republican progressives. Anyone who wants to give our citizens health care and create new green jobs has my vote. Just step out of the woodwork.

In the meantime, we should work on manufacturing progress within the Democratic party. Jill Stein isn't returning my calls, so I really have nowhere else to go.

CHAPTER 11

DO YOU WANT TO WIN ARGUMENTS OR DO YOU WANT TO MAKE THE WORLD A BETTER PLACE?

This book exists because of my mother, Kathryn. Obviously, in the very literal sense that she created me, and I created the book, but more importantly, she was my inspiration.

We're different people. I may not always be the best son, or even in the right part of the bell curve, but she's always put her whole spirit into being the best mom she can. My birth parents are divorced, and now that enough time has passed, my father has mentioned how much of the early developmental work a baby needs my mother did, which isn't easy to admit. When I was bored and lonely in middle school, she spoke with my teachers and found a gifted and talented program at a nearby college I attended on the weekends. That program helped me get into a high school that was frankly way out of my league, which helped for a college out of my league, and so on and so forth. I still look over my shoulder from time to time, expecting someone to realize I'm not supposed to be here, but no one seems to have figured it out yet.

At some point in high school or college, all of this luck got to my head, and I started (continued?) being a real brat. Going to school in DC grew my interest in politics every year, and by 2016 the election was infecting everything. While my father was a true Independent until that year, I never really took my mom seriously when she was mulling over options for the Republican primary. Maybe I just never listened.

When she was actually excited by Trump's win, it blew my mind, and then I blew up. It didn't jive with my understanding of the world. Only bad people were Trump sympathizers, but my mom really genuinely got along with everyone from every background in my diverse hometown. Why wouldn't she listen to me when I told her how wrong she was? My identity as an elitist liberal won out over my identity as a good son, and I stopped really communicating with her for longer than I'd like to admit.

I missed my mother. I grew. She didn't hold it over me even though I deserved it. Time goes on. I needed my mom more than I needed to be right.

Last year we were walking around my mother's hometown, taking a break from helping my great aunt move to a nursing home. It was a warm summer night along the Hudson River, and we were thinking about Turkish food. Passing strangers on the street, we discussed mask-wearing, and then she asked about the writing I'd been doing for myself about the pandemic. What was wild was how we were on the same page for about 80 percent of it (the wealthy were looting the Treasury while everyone else was getting the short end of the stick) before it veered off into Fox News talking points (I've known her literally my whole life. I know what kind of phrases she does and doesn't use).

We hadn't seen each other in months, so we rode that wave of reunion good cheer and kept it civil despite how quickly those conversations can get heated. It really bothers me when people don't listen to what I'm saying due to the simple fact that I'm quite needy, and so I noticed if I explained myself simply and without jumping right to the confrontational buzzwords that cause people's brains to shut down, I could get my point across. At some point during our walk home, she interrupted my ramble on the sinister liberal agenda to tell me that I should start a podcast. This is the highest compliment you can get from a white woman in her fifties.

I hate the sound of my own voice, but the thought stuck. My frustrated writings found a new direction. How do you talk to a loved one who watches Fox News? (The quick answer is to shit on Nancy Pelosi and then go from there.)

Who we are influences our political views, and our political views can influence who we are. When I reflect on the experiences that made me who I am, I realize how truly lucky I am. Lucky to have been surrounded by empathetic people who kept me from jumping off a bridge and kept me emotionally grounded. Lucky for a great public school system for my early education. Lucky that whoever was on the admissions committee at my high school showed up to work drunk the day they were reading my application. Lucky that I grew up chubby because humility is much easier to learn when you're young.

Most of the things that made me who I am were entirely out of my control. Having seen first-hand the impact that those factors can have on you means I think everyone should be afforded those opportunities. All that makes me special is having been at the right place at the right time. Everyone else has that within them too. It just needs to be nurtured to help them reach their best selves. It's my duty to do my part to help make the world a place where that can happen.

Being a progressive is about compassion. I like being right. I like winning arguments on Twitter. But that's not the goal. At a certain point, my identity as a liberal or my desire to be right got in the way of the principles that drive how I see the world. My goal is for my mother, my sister, my niece, everyone to have access to health care. Even if she doesn't agree with me, I will still speak up for my mom's right to be healthy, free, and able to pursue a happy life. America has millions of people out there like my mother, and a lot of them probably think I'm a dirty liberal at best or an idiot at worst. That's fine. They deserve good things too. When I think of these issues, I think of my mom. I'm willing to look like an idiot to fight for what's right for her, even if she disagrees with me.

Do I still succumb to those tendencies to try and win arguments for no reason other than to feel good about myself?

Absolutely, especially after a couple of drinks. But the important thing is to have your values drive what you believe and how you act, rather than the other way around. Political power or a sense of superiority are lonely goals in and of themselves but improving the quality of people's lives is something worth working toward.

One thing I've reflected on over the course of this book is how thoroughly our identities shape our thoughts. Again, this is something so basic and obvious that we don't think about it, a la a fish noticing water. It's all well and good to make fun of how rambling Trump's speech pattern is, but you run the risk of ignoring the fact that a lot of people think he talks just like them. It's an even bigger sin to admit the fact that despite being a horrible person, he's actually pretty funny. (Look me in the eyes and say that him telling a seven-year-old believing in Santa Claus is "a little marginal" and tell me it's not one of the funniest things that have happened in the White House.)

Politics is the art of winning people over to your side.

Sometimes when I would talk with my mother about climate change, I would get too caught up with spitting out facts to slow down and consider what might register with her and tell her why she should care. That's on me. Now I try to talk about why you should care even if you don't believe me.

One of the lessons of the last few years is that even if the facts are on your side and the other guy is a white supremacist, you can still lose the argument. To have more people on your side, you need people to understand what exactly you're saying.

People don't vote for the smartest person in the room, or Elizabeth Warren would be president.

One of the first questions I asked in this book is, "What does an America that works for everyone look like?" It's a question I ask in good faith because for a few decades following the New Deal it seemed like it would eventually be possible. You could say that people were always being exploited under the system by not receiving the full value of their labor, but at least all of the classes were sharing the growth.

It's become clear that there are some sick bastards who don't want an America that works for everyone, even if they aren't at the top. Dealing with them is a little above my pay grade. Most people, thankfully, are good people. The only option I can think of is to explain what the path we're on looks like, show the dangers of continuing down that path, and try to convince the people in my life of the alternative. Hopefully, you will empathize with the people you're talking to and try to do the same.

There's no map that will guide out the correct path for a more equal, just society. It's a location you get to by compass. When the compass is pointing toward fighting inequality and stewarding the planet, the short-term goals should fall in line. Better things are possible.

There's a lot on the line, but I believe in us. Good luck to us all.

ACKNOWLEDGMENTS

The ups and downs of writing a book will give you altitude sickness. I owe everything to the incredible people in my life, particularly for all of the support they've given me throughout this whole process. All of the good in these pages is attributed to them.

We made it, baby!

Thank you first and most importantly to Agnieszka Storozynski. You are the smartest person I know and one of the most caring. Nearly every good thing in my life is because of you, but I would still love you immensely, even if that weren't the case.

Thank you to Alex Storozynski for inspiring my love of stories as a child and pushing me to be curious about the world.

Thank you to Bella Storozynski for being a ball of sunshine.

Thank you to Kathryn Wowk for the reasons outlined earlier. Love you lots.

Thank you to Barbara Wellman for your wisdom, big heart, and open ears. Spending the summers with you as a kid is one of my fondest memories. I hope to be half as kind as you one day.

Thank you to Lili Davoudian for being my most important early reader and sounding board and for always willing to voice your opinion.

Thank you to Eric Koester, without whom this book wouldn't have happened.

Thank you to my incredible editors Ashley Lanuza and Michael Bailey, for your amazing input and for telling me that my early work was readable enough to keep going.

Thank you to Matt Stoller for taking the time to speak with me and cutting right to the chase with some excellent advice.

Thank you to Emmanuel Saez and Gabriel Zucman, whom I've never met but whose work shaped the framework of this book. A book about tax policy shouldn't have been so readable, but *Triumph of Injustice* is incredible.

Thank you to every teacher I've ever had, especially the ones from elementary school to middle school. I'm sure I was a pain in the class, but you taught me a lot. Big thanks to Ms. Varela and Ms. Oliver; I probably wouldn't have survived middle school without you.

Thanks to Tracy Coyne and Lauren McKeen at the Northwestern University library.

Thank you to El-P and Killer Mike of Run the Jewels. Your music helped inspire me and then served as the soundtrack to this book.

Thank you to Bernie Sanders for inspiring a political revolution based on treating people with the dignity they deserve and doing the right fuckin' thing.

Thank you to the amazing human beings I am lucky enough to call my friends. You make life worth living, especially the weirdos.

Thank you to everyone who contributed to my Indiegogo campaign: John "Jack" Larkin, Jade Wellman, Travis Cook Young, Teddy Ogilvie-Thompson, Mia Sobin, Ryan Stavarski, Dylan Farrell, Ainsley Fahey, Ideen Ashraf-Khorassa, Justin Poirier, Claire Keating, Sarah Elizabeth Stavarski, Maxwell Snyder, Seth Menghi, Neal Bakshi, Marcel Wolff, Rohan Pavuluri, Erin NaPier, Andrea Puenchera, Andrew Caetta, Michael Hyams, Hilary Hugin, Aarsh Sachdeva, Alfredo Sugawara, Joon Yang, John Ruxton, Chance Rodriguez, Ashley Graddy, Brighid Keating, Barbara Wellman, Ashley Sherman, Sarah Sutphin, Henry Hawbaker, Mary Weisenberger, Zach Ghaffari, Liam Trampota, Jabari Bullock, John Moon, Max Heald, Tiggy Valen, Jackson Smith, Cal Mullan, Austin Crouse, Samantha Williams, Daniel Sheldon, Matthew Criswell, Akinyele Jordan, Tatiana Tilearcio, Emmett Ogiony, Madeline Niebanck, Andrew Minkovitz, Hannah Gardner, Kathryn Wowk, Michael Hunter, Mary Clark Di Russo, Pamela O'Mahony, Conrad "Oliver" Everhard, Ruth Stidham, Richard Weiner, Natalie Newton, Malina Gulino, Sam Hurst, Karla Beltran, Joseph Bibbo, Renee Castagno,

Peter Bitman, Jacob Vance, Keith Selover, Joseph Lyu, Eric Koester, Diego Montemayor, Nikhil Chuchra, Christopher White, Ben Weston, Lauren Wellman, Dean Walsh, Chris Bussing, Josh Hemintakoon, Samantha Little, Robert Hersov, Joshua Zhang, James Gruetzmacher, Macy Dolan, Matteo Izzi, Maggie Mullard, Eleftherios Theodosiou, Michelle Soucy, Alex Ellison, Greg Herrigel, Kihong Ahn, Matt McDonough, Daniel Bausher-Belton, Craig Poskanzer, Alana Camina, Xina Sun, Gary Wowk, Georg Stolt-Nielsen, Arjun Venkatachalam, Kesso Lake, Daniel Ochoa, Robert Vanderpluijm, Adam Smith, Aaliyah Holcomb, Cristina Hackley, Andrew Campbell, Tiffany Kaufman, George Ward, Andrew Rondeau, Finn Meeks, Hamilton House, Nolan James Morris, Connor Pearson, Ian Foster, Chris Keating, Jennifer Thorp, Daniel Fetcho, Kent Grayson, Meghan Turner, Will Clansky, John Snyder, Ryan Toomey, Tamara Galloway, Nick Balboni, Jorge Ortiz, Mary Weisenberger, and especially Max Fiege.

Finally, thank you to the impossibly lovely Celine. You inspire me to be a better human being (and hopefully less of an asshole) every day.

APPENDIX

CHAPTER ONE

Curtin, Melanie. "Meet the 8 Men Who Control Half the World's Wealth." *Inc.com*, January 19, 2017.

International Institute for Sustainable Development. "Ending World Hunger Is within Reach: Study Finds It Will Cost Only USD 11 Billion More a Year." Accessed March 11, 2021.

Fottrell, Quentin. "Most Americans Say Their Children Will Be Worse Off." MarketWatch. 2015.

Evers-Hillstrom, Karl. "The Price of Victory Is Steep." OpenSecrets News, February 19, 2019.

Goldstein, Amy. "Income Emerges as a Major Predictor of Coronavirus Infections, along with Race." *Washington Post*. Accessed March 11, 2021.

Haider, Areeba. "The Basic Facts about Children in Poverty." Center for American Progress. Accessed March 11, 2021.

Hertel, Florian R., and Olaf Groh-Samberg. "The Relation between Inequality and Intergenerational Class Mobility in 39 Countries." *American Sociological Review* 84, no. 6 (December 1, 2019): 1099–1133.

Lee, Michelle Ye Hee. "Does Money Even Matter? And Other Questions You May Have about Bloomberg's Half-Billion-Dollar Failed Candidacy." *Washington Post*. March 4, 2020.

McGrail, Samantha, "Insulin Prices 8x Higher in the US Compared to Similar Nations." PharmaNewsIntelligence, October 12, 2020.

Sable-Smith, Bram. "Insulin's High Cost Leads to Lethal Rationing." NPR.org, September 1, 2018.

Smiljanic, Stasha. "Homelessness Statistics in the US for 2020." *Policy Advice,* February 21, 2021.

Smith, Adam B. "US Billion-Dollar Weather and Climate Disasters, 1980–Present." NOAA National Centers for Environmental Information, 2020.

University of California Television (UCTV). "George Lakoff: Moral Politics." Video, 2008.

Wenar, Leif. "John Rawls." *The Stanford Encyclopedia of Philosophy.* Metaphysics Research Lab, Stanford University. 2017.

CHAPTER TWO

Astor, Maggie. "The Electoral College Is Close. The Popular Vote Isn't." *The New York Times,* November 13, 2020.

Benner, Katie, and Michael S. Schmidt. "Barr Acknowledges Justice Dept. Has Found No Widespread Voter Fraud." *The New York Times,* December 2, 2020.

Collins, Eliza. "Les Moonves: Trump's Run Is 'Damn Good for CBS.'" *Politico,* February 2016.

Facebook's Top 10 (@FacebooksTop10). "The Top-Performing Link Posts by US Facebook Pages in the Last 24 Hours Are From: 1. Ben Shapiro 2. Go Awesome Animals 3. Fox News 4. Franklin Graham 5. Ben Shapiro 6. Ben Shapiro 7. Dan Bongino 8. Dan Bongino 9. Film 10. Fox News." Twitter, March 4, 2021, 12:08 PM.

Farley, Robert. "Trump's Rare Apology." *FactCheck.org.* December 12, 2017.

Flood, Brian. "Fox News Celebrates 19 Straight Years as Most-Watched Cable News Network." Fox News, February 2, 2021.

Halaschak, Zachary. "AOC: 'Embarrassing' for Marijuana Legalization to Be Excluded from DNC Platform." *Washington Examiner.* 2020.

Koetsier, John. "Joe Rogan Takes $100 Million to Move Podcast to Spotify, Drops Apple, YouTube." *Forbes.* Accessed March 11, 2021.

Kotch, Alex. "Koch Foundation Criticizes Turning Point USA Even as Koch Network Funds the Group." *PR Watch,* April 1, 2020.

Lakoff, George. *The ALL NEW Don't Think of an Elephant!* White River Junction, VT: Chelsea Green Publishing, 2014.

Liptak, Adam. "Supreme Court Rejects Republican Challenge to Pennsylvania Vote." *The New York Times,* December 8, 2020.

Media Monitors. "Audience Demographic Variations Are Specific to Genre and Even Individual Podcasts." *Media Monitors* (blog), March 2, 2020.

MSNBC. "Trump Campaign Gives Supporters Talking Points to Take On Liberal Relatives." *Deadline,* MSNBC. Accessed March 11, 2021.

Nuzzi, Olivia. "Donald Trump Brings Four Bill Clinton Accusers to Debate, Definitely Not Sorry About Tape." *The Daily Beast*, October 10, 2016, sec. politics.

Queally, Jon. "Trump Admits 'You'd Never Have a Republican Elected in This Country Again' If Voting Access Expanded." *Salon*, March 31, 2020.

"New Rule: Democrats Need a Coach." *Real Time with Bill Maher*. Aired May 31, 2019, on HBO.

Smith, David. "'I Don't Take Responsibility': Trump Shakes Hands and Spreads Blame over Coronavirus." *The Guardian*, March 14, 2020.

Thompson, Derek. "How Cable News Got Filthy Rich by Covering the Bejesus Out of Donald Trump." *The Atlantic*, June 17, 2016.

TYT Network, "Ben Shapiro 'Owns the Libs'... but Who Owns Him?" July 31, 2018.

CHAPTER THREE

Arakaki, Marc. "Pioneering Wireless Technology ALOHAnet Honored as Engineering Milestone." *University of Hawai'i News*, March 10, 2020.

Barroso, Amy, Kim Parker, and Jesse Bennett. "How Millennials Approach Family Life." *Pew Research Center's Social & Demographic Trends Project* (blog), May 27, 2020.

Cadogan, Tim. "GoFundMe CEO: Hello Congress, Americans Need Help and We Can't Do Your Job for You." *USA TODAY*, February 11, 2021.

Carter, Ian. "Positive and Negative Liberty." *The Stanford Encyclopedia of Philosophy*. Edited by Edward N. Zalta. Metaphysics Research Lab, Stanford University, 2019.

Fry, Richard. "For First Time in Modern Era, Living with Parents Edges Out Other Living Arrangements for 18- to 34-Year-Olds." *Pew Research Center's Social & Demographic Trends Project* (blog), May 24, 2016.

Lakoff, George. *The ALL NEW Don't Think of an Elephant!* White River Junction, VT: Chelsea Green Publishing, 2014.

McKay, Mary Fae, David McKay, and Michael Duke. "Space Resources: Sourcing and Sustaining Optimum Financing." National Aeronautics and Space Administration Scientific and Technical Information Program. Accessed March 5, 2021

Roberts, Karen. "UD Inventors of Touch Imaging Interface Technology Inducted as NAI Fellows." *UDaily*, May 27, 2014.

Giridharadas, Anand. Interview by Trevor Noah. *The Daily Show*, Comedy Central, October 1, 2019. https://www.cc.com/video/jonhru/the-daily-show-with-trevor-noah-anand-giridharadas-winners-take-all-and-the-paradox-of-elite-philanthropy-extended-interview?xrs=synd_twitter_100219_tds_77.

Wilkinson, Amy. "Why Millennials Aren't Starting Businesses (and Why That's a Problem)." *Wall Street Journal*, August 25, 2015.

Zaveri, Mihir. "Monsanto Weedkiller Roundup Was 'Substantial Factor' in Causing Man's Cancer, Jury Says." *The New York Times*, March 20, 2019, sec. Business.

Zimmermann, Kim Ann and Jesse Emspak. "Internet History Timeline: ARPANET to the World Wide Web." *Live Science*, June 27, 2017.

CHAPTER FOUR

Baker, Dean. "Job Lock and Employer-Provided Health Insurance: Evidence from the Literature." *AARP Public Policy Institute*, n.d., 41.

Bureau of Labor Statistics. "Employment Recovery in the Wake of the COVID-19 Pandemic: Monthly Labor Review: US Bureau of Labor Statistics." February 2020.

Cecere, David. "New Study Finds 45,000 Deaths Annually Linked to Lack of Health Coverage." *Harvard Gazette* (blog), September 17, 2009.

Committee for a Responsible Federal Budget. "American Health Care: Health Spending and the Federal Budget." Committee for a Responsible Federal Budget, May 16, 2018.

Dunleavy, Brian. "RAND: US Brand-Name Drug Prices Nearly Three Times Higher than Other Countries." *UPI*, January 28, 2021.

Feldscher, Karen. "US Pays More for Health Care with Worse Population Health Outcomes." *Harvard Gazette* (blog), March 13, 2018.

Garfield, Rachel, Gary Claxton, and Anthony Damico. "Eligibility for ACA Health Coverage Following Job Loss." *KFF* (blog), May 13, 2020.

Hackett, Mallory. "The Average Cost of Hospital Care for COVID-19 Ranges from $51,000 to $78,000 Based on Age." *Healthcare Finance News*. November 5, 2020.

Herman, Bob. "The Sky-High Pay of Health Care CEOs." *Axios*, July 24, 2017.

Integrated Benefits Institute. "Poor Health Costs US Employers $530 Billion." *Integrated Benefits Institute* (blog), November 15, 2018.

Kenton, Will. "Should We Bring Back the Glass-Steagall Act?" *Investopedia*. Accessed March 11, 2021.

Khan Academy. "Shays's Rebellion (Article)." *Khan Academy*. Accessed March 11, 2021.

Konish, Lorie. "This Is the Real Reason Most Americans File for Bankruptcy." *CNBC*, February 11, 2019.

Leonhardt, Megan. "Nearly 1 in 4 Americans Are Skipping Medical Care Because of the Cost." *CNBC*, March 12, 2020.

McDermott, Daniel, Cynthia Cox, Robin Rudowitz, and Rachel Garfield. "How Has the Pandemic Affected Health Coverage in the US?" *KFF* (blog), December 9, 2020.

National Aeronautics and Space Administration. *FY 2020 Spending Plan for Appropriations Provided by P.L. 116–93 and P.L. 116–136*. Accessed March 5, 2021.

Nationmaster. "Cuba vs. United States Health Stats Compared." Accessed March 11, 2021.

Palosky, Craig, and Sue Ducat. "Benchmark Employer Survey Finds Average Family Premiums Now Top $20,000." *KFF* (blog), September 25, 2019.

Warren, Elizabeth. "Health Care Is a Human Right." Warren Campaign. Accessed March 11, 2021.

Elizabeth Warren. "My First Term Plan for Reducing Health Care Costs in America." Warren Campaign. Accessed March 11, 2021.

Winsor, Morgan. "US Life Expectancy Drops 1 Year in First Half of 2020 amid Coronavirus Pandemic, CDC Says." ABC News, February 18, 2021.

Zoellner, Danielle. "Woman Who Needed Facial Reconstruction after Bear Attack Says She Was Forced to 'Prostitute Herself on TV' to Survive." *The Independent*, March 6, 2020.

CHAPTER FIVE

Blitz, Matt. "When America's Infrastructure Saved Democracy." *Popular Mechanics*, January 23, 2017.

Brosig, Max, Parker Frawley, Molly Jahn, Michael Marsicek, Aubrey Paris, Matthew Rose, Amar Shambaljamts, and Nicole Thomas. "Implications of Climate Change for the US Army." *United States Army War College*, n.d., 52.

Carnevale, Anthony, Megan Fasules, Michael Quinn, and Kathryn Peltier Campbell. "Born to Win, Schooled to Lose: Why Equally Talented Students Don't Get Equal Chances to Be All They Can Be." *CEW Georgetown* (blog), 2019.

Deeben, John. "Family Experiences and New Deal Relief." National Archives, August 15, 2016.

Demographia. "US Population: From 1900." Accessed March 12, 2021.

DiChristopher, Tom. "Climate Disasters Cost $650 Billion over Three Years: Morgan Stanley." CNBC, February 14, 2019.

Economist Intelligence Unit. "Global Economy Will Be 3 Percent Smaller by 2050 Due to Lack of Climate Resilience." Economist Intelligence Unit, November 20, 2019.

Ocasio-Cortez, Alexandria. "Text-H.Res.109-116th Congress (2019-2020): Recognizing the Duty of the Federal Government to Create a Green New Deal." Webpage, February 12, 2019.

Stoller, Matt. *Goliath: The 100-Year War Between Monopoly Power and Democracy.* New York: Simon and Schuster, 2019.

World Integrated Trade Solution. "United States Textiles and Clothing Imports by Country 2018 | WITS Data." Accessed March 12, 2021.

CHAPTER SIX

Varoufakis, Yanis. *Talking to My Daughter About the Economy or, How Capitalism Works—and How It Fails.* Translated by Yanis Varoufakis and Jacob Moe. New York: Farrar, Straus and Giroux, 2017.

CHAPTER SEVEN

Berger, Sarah. "Warren Buffett Has Been Making the Same Salary for Decades—and It's Surprisingly Low." CNBC, March 19, 2018.

Bregman, Rutger. *Utopia for Realists: How We Can Build the Ideal World.* New York: Back Bay Books, 2017.

Cohen, Seth. "US Workers Have Lost $1.3 Trillion—So Why Is Stimulus on Hold?" *Forbes*, May 5, 2020.

Collins, Chuck. "Updates: Billionaire Wealth, US Job Losses and Pandemic Profiteers." Inequality.org. Accessed March 12, 2021.

Ghilarducci, Teresa. "Most Americans Don't Have A Real Stake In The Stock Market." *Forbes*, August 31, 2020.

Hope, David, and Julian Limberg. "The Economic Consequences of Major Tax Cuts for the Rich." Monograph. London, UK: London School of Economics and Political Science, December 2020.

Ingraham, Christopher. "Analysis | The Top Tax Rate Has Been Cut Six Times Since 1980—Usually with Democrats' Help." *Washington Post.* February 27, 2019

Institute on Taxation and Economic Policy. "Fairness Matters: A Chart Book on Who Pays State and Local Taxes." ITEP. Accessed March 12, 2021.

Institute on Taxation and Economic Policy. "Florida: Who Pays? 6th Edition." Institute on Taxation and Economic Policy. Accessed March 12, 2021.

Li, Yun. "Warren Buffett's Net Worth Surpasses $100 Billion for the First Time as Berkshire Shares Hit Record." CNBC, March 11, 2021.

Influencer Marketing Hub. "OnlyFans Statistics—Users, Revenue and Usage Stats." December 4, 2020.

Mishel, Lawrence, and Jessica Schieder. "CEO Pay Remains High Relative to the Pay of Typical Workers and High-Wage Earners." Economic Policy Institute. July 20, 2017.

Saez, Emmanuel, and Gabriel Zucman. *The Triumph of Injustice: How the Rich Dodge Taxes and How to Make Them Pay*. New York: W.W. Norton & Company, 2019.

Scheve, Kenneth, and David Stasavage. "Taxing the Rich: Fairness and Fiscal Sacrifice over Two Centuries." Ford School at the University of Michigan, October 29, 2015.

Scheve, Kenneth, and David Stasavage. "The Conscription of Wealth: Mass Warfare and the Demand for Progressive Taxation." UK: Cambridge University Press on behalf of the International Organization Foundation, 2010.

US Bureau of Labor Statistics. "Consumer Expenditures in 2018." US Bureau of Labor Statistics Reports, May 2020.

CHAPTER EIGHT

Americans for Tax Fairness. "Congress Gives Rich & Powerful Christmas Bonuses through Expensive Tax Breaks in COVID Relief Bill." *Americans for Tax Fairness* (blog). Accessed March 12, 2021.

Bregman, Rutger. *Utopia for Realists: How We Can Build the Ideal World*. New York: Back Bay Books, 2017.

Celebrity Net Worth. "Cardi B Net Worth," January 30, 2020.

Cochrane, Emily. "Democrats Narrow Stimulus Payments as Biden Works to Keep Aid Plan on Track." *The New York Times*, March 4, 2021.

Day, Nate. "What Is the Kardashian-Jenner Family's Net Worth?" *FOXBusiness*, Fox Business, January 6, 2021.

Economic Policy Institute. "The Productivity–Pay Gap." *Economic Policy Institute* (blog). Accessed March 12, 2021.

Gale, William G. "Did the 2017 Tax Cut—the Tax Cuts and Jobs Act—Pay for Itself?" *Brookings* (blog), February 14, 2020.

Herman, Bob. "Corporate America Reaps Windfalls from Coronavirus Tax Breaks." *Axios*, June 18, 2020.

Horsley, Scott. "After Two Years, Trump Tax Cuts Have Failed to Deliver on GOP's Promises." NPR.org, December 20, 2019.

Greenwald, Daniel, Martin Lettau, and Sydney Ludvigson. "How the Wealth Was Won: Factors Shares as Market Fundamentals." Cambridge, MA: National Bureau of Economic Research, April 2019.

Kochhar, Rakesh. "Unemployment Rose Higher in Three Months of -19 Than It Did in Two Years of the Great Recession." *Pew Research Center* (blog), June 11, 2020.

JUST Capital. "The JUST Capital Rankings on Corporate Tax Reform." *JUST Capital* (blog). Accessed March 12, 2021.

Pemberton, Justin, dir. *Capital in the Twenty-First Century*. 2019; General Film Corporation, Upside Productions, Netflix, 2019.

Ngo, Madeleine. "Small Businesses Are Quietly Dying by the Thousands during the Coronavirus Pandemic." *Chicago Tribune*, chicagotribune.com, August 8, 2020.

Schaal, Eric. "These Companies Laid Off Large Numbers of Employees after Taking Trump's Tax Cuts." *Showbiz Cheat Sheet* (blog), April 12, 2018.

Troise, Damian. "US Companies Tax Windfall Fuels Record Share Buybacks." AP NEWS, April 4, 2019.

Warren, Elizabeth. "Ultra-Millionaire Tax." Warren Campaign. Accessed March 12, 2021.

CHAPTER NINE

Duffy, Kate. "Biden Tells Georgia Voters That $2,000 Stimulus Checks Will Never Arrive If Republicans Win Senate Runoffs." *Business Insider*. Accessed March 13, 2021.

Howe, Amy. "Details on Shelby County v. Holder: In Plain English." *SCOTUSblog* (blog), June 25, 2013.

Pauwels, Jacques R. "Profits 'Über Alles!' American Corporations and Hitler." Edited by Edwin Black, Walter Hofer, Herbert R. Reginbogin, Reinhold Billstein, Karola Fings, Anita Kugler, and Nicholas Levis. *Labour / Le Travail* 51 (2003): 223–49.

Paxton, Robert O. *The Anatomy of Fascism*. Published simultaneously in New York and Toronto: Vintage Books, 2004.

Roosevelt, Franklin Delano. "Message to Congress on Curbing Monopolies | The American Presidency Project." The American Presidency Project. Accessed March 13, 2021.

Some More News. *Trumpism Is Just a Synonym for Fascism-SOME MORE NEWS*, 18:36, Video, 2018. https://www.youtube.com/watch?v=fIN8oxnw__I&t=690s.

Stoller, Matt. *Goliath: The 100-Year War between Monopoly Power and Democracy*. New York: Simon and Schuster, 2019.

Sullivan, Andy. "Southern US States Have Closed 1,200 Polling Places in Recent Years: Rights Group." Reuters, September 10, 2019.

Taylor, Bill. "What Breaking the Four-Minute Mile Taught Us about the Limits of Conventional Thinking." *Harvard Business Review*, March 9, 2018.

Venkataramanan, Meena. "Trump Is the 'Most Effective Uprooter of Liberalism': Newt Gingrich Talks GOP, Midterms, Space." ABC News. Accessed March 13, 2021.

CHAPTER TEN

Berman, Russell. "Boehner Says No Thanks to Another Conservative Revolt." *The Atlantic*, September 25, 2015.

Bowman, Karlyn and Jennifer Marsico., "As the Tea Party Turns Five, It Looks a Lot Like the Conservative Base." *Forbes*. February 24, 2014.

Castronuovo, Celine. "Half of Republicans in New Poll Say Election Was 'Rigged,' Stolen from Trump." Text. *The Hill*, November 18, 2020.

Fahrenthold, David A., and Katie Zezima. "For Ted Cruz, the 2013 Shutdown Was a Defining Moment." *Washington Post*, February 16, 2016, sec. Politics.

Gallup. "Presidential Approval Ratings—Donald Trump." Gallup, November 16, 2016. Accessed March 13, 2021.

Gilens, Martin, and Benjamin I. Page. "Testing Theories of American Politics: Elites, Interest Groups, and Average Citizens." *Perspectives on Politics* 12, no. 3 (September 2014): 564–81.

Goldmacher, Shane. "An Upset in the Making: Why Joe Crowley Never Saw Defeat Coming." *The New York Times*, June 27, 2018, sec. New York.

Goodman, Joseph. "Libertarians by the Numbers: A Demographic, Religious, and Political Profile." *PRRI* (blog). Accessed March 13, 2021.

Lee, MJ. "Donald Trump Courts Tea Party at Nashville Straw Poll." *CNN Politics*, CNN, August 29, 2015.

Lizza, Ryan. "The War Inside the Republican Party." *The New Yorker*. December 4, 2015

Mangan, Dan. "Trump Claims He Has 'No Financial Interests in Saudi Arabia'—but He Makes Lots of Money from It." CNBC, October 16, 2018.

Marans, Daniel, and Hayley Miller. "Bernie Sanders Campaign Says It Raised $46.5 Million in February." *HuffPost*, Accessed March 12, 2021

Markey Campaign, "About Ed | US Senator Ed Markey of Massachusetts." Accessed March 13, 2021.

McGrath, Ben. "The Movement." *The New Yorker*. February 1, 2010.

Nyhan, Brendan, "Beware Context-Free Election Analysis." *HuffPost*. December 4, 2010.

O'Connell, Patrick M. "Businesswoman Marie Newman's Victory in Democratic Primary Ends Decades of Lipinski Reign." *Chicago Tribune*, March 18, 2020.

Page, Benjamin I., Larry M. Bartels, and Jason Seawright. "Democracy and the Policy Preferences of Wealthy Americans." *Perspectives on Politics* 11, no. 1 (March 2013): 51–73.

Pew Research, "Americans' Views of Government: Low Trust, but Some Positive Performance Ratings." *Pew Research Center-US Politics & Policy* (blog), September 14, 2020.

Rauch, Jonathan. "Group Think: Inside the Tea Party's Collective Brain." Accessed March 13, 2021.

Reich, Robert B. *The System: Who Rigged It, How We Fix It*. New York: Alfred A. Knopf, 2020.

Scott, Michelle P. "Explaining Biden's Tax Plan." Investopedia. Accessed March 13, 2021.

Shear, Michael. "Ryan Brings the Tea Party to the Ticket." *The New York Times*, August 12, 2012.

Siddiqui, Sabrina, Ben Jacobs, and Tom McCarthy. "House Speaker John Boehner to Resign after Battle with Conservatives." *The Guardian*, September 25, 2015.

Solender, Andrew. "106 House Republicans Support Trump-Backed Lawsuit to Overturn Election." *Forbes*. December 10, 2020.

The Center for Responsive Politics, "Rep. Alexandria Ocasio-Cortez-Campaign Finance Summary." OpenSecrets. Accessed March 13, 2021.

Pelosi, Nancy. Interview by Jon Stewart. "Exclusive-Nancy Pelosi Extended Interview Pt. 2." *The Daily Show with Jon Stewart*, Comedy Central, January 30, 2014.

The Heritage Foundation. *CNBC's Rick Santelli's Chicago Tea Party*, 2009.

Weisman, Jonathan. "GOP in Lead in Final Lap." *Wall Street Journal*, October 20, 2010, sec. US.

Yancey-Bragg, N'dea and William Cummings. "Black Lives Matter Activist Cori Bush Becomes Missouri's First Black Congresswoman." *USA TODAY*. November 4, 2020.

Made in the USA
Middletown, DE
22 June 2021